<u>Welcome
to
Dumbfckistan</u>

<u>The
Dumbed-Down
Disinformed
Dysfunctional
Disunited
States
Of
America</u>

<u>IAN GURVITZ</u>

ISBN-13: 978-1523313952

ISBN-10: 15233-13951

Copyright: 2016 Ian Gurvitz

Cover Photo: copyright Christophe BOISSON

American flag photo: copyright natrot

CONTENTS

FOREWORD

CHAPTER ONE -- DUMBF✲CKISTAN -- An introduction.

CHAPTER TWO -- DUMBF✲CK BELIEFS -- We think we're the cosmic shit.

CHAPTER THREE -- DUMBF✲CK FREEDOM -- Atlas sharted.

CHAPTER FOUR -- DUMBF✲CK POWER -- Happiness is a warm gun.

CHAPTER FIVE -- DUMBF✲CK CULTURE -- Bread and circuses.

CHAPTER SIX -- DUMBF✲CK STATES OF MIND – A Flyover Analysis.

CHAPTER SEVEN -- DUMBF✲CK POLITICS – Disinformation nation.

CHAPTER EIGHT -- DUMBF✲CK RELIGION – PART 1 Deconstruction. PART 2 Resurrection.

CHAPTER NINE -- DUMBF✲CK HABITS – Smoking: A memoir.

CHAPTER TEN -- DUMBF✲CKISTAN: THE FUTURE -- Life, Liberty, Happiness. The 2016 Election: A Battle for the Heart, Mind, and Soul of America.

AFTERWORD – TRUMPOCALYPSE NOW.

"I have a foreboding of an America in my children's or grandchildren's time – when the United States is a service and information economy; when nearly all the manufacturing industries have slipped away to other countries; when awesome technological powers are in the hands of a very few, and no one representing the public interest can even grasp the issues; when the people have lost the ability to set their own agenda or knowledgeably question those in authority; when, clutching our crystals and nervously consulting our horoscopes, our critical faculties in decline, unable to distinguish between what feels good and what's true, we slide, almost without noticing, back into superstition and darkness… The dumbing down of America is most evident in the slow decay of substantive content in the enormously influential media, the 30-seond sound bites… lowest common denominator programming, credulous presentations on pseudoscience and superstition, but especially a kind of celebration of ignorance."

Carl Sagan
The Demon-Haunted World, Science as a Candle in the Dark
Published 1975

6

FOREWORD

Warning: this book is an unapologetic liberal screed about the deteriorating state of our national dialogue, which is dragging down our culture, our politics, and our lives. It contains strong opinions, snarky comments, and gratuitous insults directed at people and ideas I disagree with, disrespect and, in some cases, despise.

What Carl Sagan wrote over forty years ago has proven to be not just eerily prescient, but almost an understatement of how deep into the intellectual muck we've sunk. Although the Western philosophical tradition may be grounded in a Socratic search for truth, American political life has devolved into a mosh pit of willful ignorance, talking points, disinformation, and lies, while the culture has descended into a celebration of the dumbest common denominator. Burning Man for the brain dead.

There has always been an element of stupidity in America, only now it's become a valid intellectual stance. Fact has been relegated to just another opinion. Voices that, at one time in our history, would have been laughed off the national stage have now been afforded mainstream legitimacy. Idiotic remarks that would have been walked back when the speaker sobered up are now backed up with even more bluster than when they were uttered. Even racist and sexist taunts proudly ride in under the false banner of flouting political correctness. And it's all been spearheaded by Rupert Murdoch taking a giant shit in the mouth of the American conversation with Fox News. Face it: when Bill O'Reilly is the philosopher king of your network, you have a serious credibility problem.

Don't get me wrong – I love America, although, I'm not in love with it. I don't get a case of red, white and blue balls every time I see a waving flag, or some country singer belting out the national anthem. That kind of emotional patriotism is about symbols and pageantry, not ideas.

I do, however, have a deep respect for American democracy and the philosophical principles on which it was founded. Even when it's being gamed, lobbied, bought, sold, bribed, horse-traded, perverted and subverted it's still, as Churchill put it, "the worst form of government, except for all the others." Despite all the scandals and corruption in our history, we've still managed an orderly transfer of power over the last 240 years. Given the dark side of the human heart, and the ultra-violence of which we humans are capable, that's a pretty decent record.

Yet, as vital as our democracy is, at the moment it's on intellectual life support, as private interests pollute the air with false narratives crafted to mislead a gullible public. It's not the Affordable Care Act. It's "Obamacare!" There's no climate change. There's the "climate change debate." When 99% of the world's scientists agree that burning fossil fuels is adversely affecting the planet, and 10,883 out of 10,885 peer-reviewed papers confirm it, and yet a United States Senator steps on to the floor and attempts to rebut the facts by holding up a snowball, we have officially entered The Shithead Zone.

But the fault doesn't only lie in the messaging. It lies in the fact that too many of us are dumb, and easily manipulated. We never look through the message to root out the agenda. Politicians or their surrogates pop on news shows making "fact-based" claims that fly in the face of reality, and we lap it up because we're dazzled by anyone who confidently tosses around a few numbers. As Mark Twain put it: "There are three kinds of lies: lies, damned lies, and statistics."

I didn't set out to write a book. I just followed the course of our political dialogue until the mind-numbing stupidity and shameless mendacity became so overwhelming it was either stroke out, pop a Xanax, scream at the TV, or scream at my laptop.

Research was easy – I didn't do any. I just read the news and watched TV, absorbing the conversation and taking note of what ads and talking points popped up over and over. Of who was saying what, and why. I've included news items from a variety of sources, as they not only serve as a barometer on our behavior, but are indicative of the way we think. They reveal first principles and uncritically held assumptions about the world, and our place in it.

And to make sure my frustrations weren't just visceral reactions to what I was reading and hearing, I Googled, and went wherever the links took me, whether it was to traditional sources like *The New York Times, L.A. Times, Washington Post, Wall Street Journal, New York Daily News,* CNN, or MSNBC, or sites such as *The Huffington Post, The Daily Beast, The Atlantic, Salon, Politico, Bloomberg News, Yahoo News,* or *BuzzFeed.* I also drew from a variety of websites and blogs, and even took a few side trips to Wikipedia.

Don't look for footnotes; there aren't any. No bibliography either. You want to fact check it, be my guest. If I found anything that confirmed my point of view, I included it. And if I discovered articles that contradicted my take on things, I simply followed the time-honored journalistic tradition of Fox News: I distorted them out of all proportion, or completely ignored them.

CHAPTER ONE

DUMBF✶CKISTAN

AN INTRODUCTION

"Fat, drunk, and stupid is no way to go through life, son."
Dean Wormer

America is retarded. Now, before the Thought Police loses its self-righteous shit, let me clarify: the transitive verb *to retard* means to delay or hold back, in the sense of hindering an object or person's development or progress. If a child is born with a particular condition, let's say Down syndrome, then call it what it is: Down syndrome; the result of abnormal cell division involving a particular chromosome, most often during the development of the sperm or egg cell. It's a biological phenomenon that shouldn't result in labeling that person disabled, handicapped, or even differently abled, which is one of those feel-good neologisms designed to paint a happy face on a serious condition. I guarantee no kid born with that chromosomal abnormality looks in the mirror and thinks, "Man, I am one lucky, differently abled motherfucker." Although the fact that they seem to be constantly smiling makes me wonder if they experience the sheer joy of being alive in a way few of us ever know.

Still, that person has a built-in excuse for not playing professional football or teaching physics at M.I.T. Someone born what we call normal does not. Normal people have no such justification for their arrested intellectual development other than ignorance, fear, superstition, prejudice, a stubborn resistance to new ideas, or a personal or political agenda that necessitates casting doubt on things most intelligent people accept as fact. Instead of searching for truth, they embrace stupidity and wear it as a badge of honor. Reduced to its simplest form: Trig Palin is a pleasant young man with Down syndrome. Sarah Palin is retarded.

Too harsh? Consider the fact that this preening, power-hungry nincompoop believed a creator of the universe wanted her to run for national office. Consider that her stump speeches consisted of rambling, schizophasic shriek-fests delivered in a voice that sounded like a dolphin that got its dick slammed in a car door. Consider that John McCain picked her solely as a political stunt, yet they barnstormed the country campaigning under a banner that read "Country First" -- a perverse irony that was lost on most Americans at the time, and on the media. Though even more diabolical than Palin's vainglorious, Lady Macbeth-like ambition was the fact that she intimately knew her limitations and still thought she'd been anointed by God to lead the nation -- the mark of the true megalomaniac.

Yet, despite her non-stop gaffes and imbecilic answers to straightforward questions, on Election Day McCain/Palin received fifty-nine million, nine hundred and forty-eight thousand, three hundred and twenty-three votes. That means that 59,948,323 Americans -- 45.7% of the voting public -- with enough brain power to dress themselves, have coffee, leave the house and drive to a polling station actually pulled the lever to make this person Vice President of the United States. Now, I'm all for hiring the disabled but, had they won that election, Palin and her clan of snowbillies would have invaded D.C., and that clucking imbecile would have been one malfunctioning defibrillator away from possessing the nuclear launch codes.

(Take a moment to ponder the notion of Sarah Palin with nuclear strike capabilities. I don't recall if she ever used the word "nuclear," or if she pronounced it *nuke-u-lar*, like our former president. And while I've almost blocked the psychotic episode of the Bush years out of my mind, at times I get hit with the recurring nightmare that Cheney convinced W. to launch a first strike, and life on Earth was wiped out by *nuke-u-lar* radiation. Insult to injury, Armageddon-style.)

Unfortunately, Ms. Palin is hardly the only passenger on the intellectual short bus. Going right from her Election Day loss, she immediately became the hard-core right's drum majorette, leading a parade of folksy, old-timey stupidity into the American conversation. And that stupidity has taken root, not merely as another side in the debate, but in many respects, setting the narrative. It not only laid the groundwork for the Tea Party, but has infected all branches of government, from the lowliest Texas school board idiot who thinks the Earth is 6000 years old, right up to a late Supreme Court Justice.

In a 2014 interview with *New York Magazine*, senior Associate Justice Antonin Scalia stated his belief that there is an actual devil. Not a mythical creature representing the dark side of the human heart, but an actual, malevolent entity living in a fiery netherworld who, like some Bond villain holding a pitchfork instead an albino pussycat, is actually plotting to corrupt mankind. This was stated with confidence, even arrogance, by a man who made decisions affecting the lives of 325 million Americans and, by extension, the world. And yet there wasn't a single "what the fuck?!" from anyone in government, the press, or from any of his colleagues on the Court. No public outrage or call for an evaluation of his sanity and fitness to hold office. Had he shown up on the first Monday in October wearing nothing but tin foil underwear, claiming it was his only protection against aliens trying to steal his precious bodily essences, there might have been talk of a psych eval. Despite the fact that a Supreme Court Justice can be impeached for treason, bribery and other high crimes and misdemeanors, apparently being delusional doesn't make the cut. Maybe the problem is that 58% of Americans also believe in the devil. I guess it's tough to recognize insanity when you're living in the asylum.

But these are just two examples of the rampant stupidity that has metastasized throughout the country. The constitutionally protected free speech that entitles every American to express their opinion has devolved into the notion that all opinions carry equal weight, simply because they are deeply held, and passionately expressed. And not just by some morbidly obese high school dropout proudly holding a misspelled sign, but by our elected officials. Some recent examples:

* A candidate running for president in 2012 referred to higher education as "mind control" and "indoctrination." He ran again in 2016.

* A former Governor and 2012 presidential contender blamed the separation of church and state on Satan. He also sought to solve his state's drought problem by asking its citizens to pray for rain. He ran again in 2016.

* A 2012 presidential contender claimed, "there's violence in Israel because Jesus is coming soon."

* A Georgia congressman claimed that evolution and the Big Bang Theory were "lies straight from the pit of Hell," adding "Earth is about 9,000 years old and was created in six days, per the Bible." He's a physician, and a high-ranking member of the House Science Committee.

* From another member of the House Science Committee: "Prehistoric climate change could have been caused by dinosaur flatulence."

* From the Chairman of the Senate Environment and Public Works Committee: "Global warming isn't real, God is in control of the world."

* A former Speaker of the House -- a born-again Christian, and convicted felon – declared, " One thing Americans seem to forget is that God wrote the Constitution."

* The Lt. Governor of a southern state claimed that Yoga may result in satanic possession.

* A Southern senator claimed, "video games represent a bigger problem than guns, because video games affect people."

* A California state representative proudly stated: "Guns are used to defend our property and our families and our freedom, and they are absolutely essential to living the way God intended for us to live."

* Another California representative suggested that abortion was to blame for the state's drought.

* From a Texas representative: "The great flood is an example of climate change. And that certainly wasn't because mankind overdeveloped hydrocarbon energy."

* An Oklahoma representative said: "Just because the Supreme Court rules on

something doesn't necessarily mean that that's constitutional."

* From another Texas representative: "We know Al Qaeda has camps on the Mexican border. We have people that are trained to act Hispanic when they are radical Islamists."

* A South Carolina State representative, commenting on the Supreme Court's legalization of gay marriage said, "The devil is taking control of this land and we're not stopping him!"

It would be one thing if these were just the incoherent ramblings of some trailer park yokel, snarly bar drunk, or raging street-corner psycho. But they're the soberly expressed opinions of powerful government officials who make decisions that affect the course of our lives. And no one's hitting the panic button.

But the problem isn't just a few frighteningly dumb politicians. The problem is they represent a frighteningly dumb electorate. The reason Louis Gohmert is a United States Congressman is that 180,000 Gohmers and Gohmettes in Texas' First District pulled the lever to send his bald-headed goober ass to D.C. Mr. Shitkicker goes to Washington. Apparently, it takes a village full of idiots to elect a village idiot.

Sadly, with a few notable exceptions, the mainstream media, traditionally the voice of reason and healthy skepticism, is almost useless. As heads in a corporate media Hydra they're either too skittish about being labeled as biased to properly ridicule the Gohmers of the world, or too eager to air their ramblings to gin up a little on-camera controversy.

In the spring of 2011, a Gainesville, Florida mutant calling himself Pastor Terry Jones, of the Dove World Outreach, threatened to burn a copy of the Koran, and the media flocked to his backwater swamp of a church to whip up some post-9/11, anti-Muslim hysteria. A simple look at his '70s era Oakland Raider moustache should have outed him as bona fide relignoramus. Yet reporters from legitimate news organizations raced to Florida and stuck cameras and microphones in his face. The media attention gave Jones a legitimacy he in no way deserved, so he was never exposed as just some self-aggrandizing, publicity hungry clown. Or better yet, ignored.

The media flogged this story non-stop, building the tension into a "will he or won't he burn the Koran" hysteria. Eventually he did burn the Koran, which would have been fine if that had been the end of the story. A moron burned a book. Big deal. Considering the intelligence level involved, it's a miracle he didn't deep-fry it and eat it. Unfortunately, that wasn't the end of the story. The book burning, broadcast worldwide, lead to hundreds of demonstrators in Afghanistan attacking a United Nations compound, killing seven, and beheading two workers.

And then there's trial porn. In July 2013, the George Zimmerman "stand your ground" murder trial became the O.J./Rodney King trial of its day. Even though both Egypt and Syria were imploding, on MSNBC it was all trial, all the time. Of course, the fact that it touched on our lingering, virulent racism, as well as our quasi-phallic obsession with guns gave news organizations cover to dwell on it obsessively. Not that it wasn't an important story, but it also played right into the media's trial porn ratings lust, which sends them flocking to cover the two-headed snake of the week.

Which brings us to Trump -- someone who seems to live his life based on the Oscar Wilde line: "There is only one thing in life worse than being talked about, and that is not being talked about." Trump kicked off his 2016 presidential run with the outrageous claim that the Mexican government is sending us rapists. Like it's 1980 and Castro's opening the jails. And exactly how did Mexico put out the word to the rapist community, an ad on *El Craigslist*?

> *Te gusta rape?*
> *Quieres vivir en los Ustados Unidos?*
> *Llame 555-RAPE.*
> *Llame ahora!*

    In a sane society, he would have been laughed off the stage. Yet, the media covered him incessantly. It's like a 5-year-old ran into a roomful of adults and whizzed on the carpet, but instead of being scolded and sent off to bed, the adults said "fascinating, sit down, tell us more."

    Before Trump opened his mouth, his candidacy was a joke. After he spoke, it became a sick joke. One hateful, moronic utterance catapulted him to the top of Republican polls, as the media struggled to comprehend this seemingly incomprehensible phenomenon. Then the polls themselves became news. Suddenly, Trump's snarky smirk was everywhere. The more stupid shit he said, the more airtime he got. The constant coverage put him on an infomercial-like TV loop, as he went from the guy in the circus who mucks up after the elephant parade, to the ringmaster. And the media played right into it. Or, to be accurate, he played the media. And it worked. Trump and his mouth were off and running. Said one supporter, "I believe he is the man God has chosen to bring America back."

    It seems the schmucks of the country had a new king, one who could confer legitimacy on himself by funding his own campaign. And in modern politics, just as in high-stakes poker, the only requirement for getting in the game is having the cash for the buy-in. And Trump can pay his own way. Not the case with the remaining GOP candidates, who've been chasing down millions in PAC money and private support. With all the love they're getting, the Koch Brothers must feel like a couple of rich cowboys at the Moonlite Bunny Ranch.

    And it's all been sanctioned by the Supreme Court's 2010 decision in *Citizens United*, affirming that corporations are people. Really? Ever see a corporation eat a meal? Drive a car? Make love? Marry? Have kids? No? Then not people. Q.E.D. Pre-*Citizens United* can you cite one example of any individual in a corporation who was forbidden by law to express his or her opinion? And post-*Citizens United*, is it the entire corporation that decides how to spend that money? Or is it just the CEO or board of directors? Perhaps Mitt Romney was disingenuous when he said that corporations are people, too. It now seems to have gone one ominous step further: corporations are the new people.

    The freedom we love to crow about involved breaking free from a foreign monarch and proclaiming self-governance as a human right. Yet some two-and-a-half centuries later, we seem to be sliding into oligarchy, as corporations, billionaires, super PACs, and partisan think tanks attempt to turn government into a democratically themed shadow play. Electoral politics has become a magic act -- the misdirection coming in the form of advertising. Much to the delight of television networks and local stations, over $2 billion was spent on ads in 2012. More will be spent in the 2016 presidential election, much of it used to run spots infused with cleverly crafted talking points and dog whistle sound bites, all designed to push our buttons or stoke our fears. And they all come wrapped in the flag, as good lies do. There's an adage in advertising: "if you have nothing to say – sing it." In modern politics it's: "if you have nothing to say -- lie about it, stick it in a 30-second spot, and run it fifty times a day."

Yet, ultimately, the problem isn't the ads. The problem is that they work. And they work because we're dumb, and easily manipulated. We've gone from the low-information voter, to the no-information voter, to the anti-information voter; from an informed electorate to an inflamed electorate. We park our fat asses in front of the TV and uncritically absorb whatever comes out of it. And given our political affiliations, we only go to those news sources that reinforce our positions.

No one thinks outside their particular echo chamber. No one thinks, period. We believe and follow. We've lost any sense of healthy skepticism. No one asks why the same political spot airs ten times a day. Why the presentation is so dark, the voice over so ominous. Why the message is so simplistic, broken down into good and evil. Or why every member of a certain political party repeats the same stock phrases on the floor of Congress or when responding to a reporter's question, and whether that single-minded repetition is intended to virtually hypnotize us into a certain way of thinking. Or voting.

Then there's our popular entertainment. Movies have gone from an art form that reflected our lives to a series of hyper-merchandised cartoons, action films featuring fast cars, big tits, and big guns, and superhero movies designed for children, adults with children, and adults with the minds of children.

As for TV, while cable channels like HBO, Showtime, AMC, F/X, Comedy Central, and IFC, as well as streaming services like Amazon, Netflix, and Hulu, are spearheading a creative revolution not just in original content, but in how that content is delivered, they still reach a relatively small number of Americans. For the most part, network TV, with its singing, dancing, and weight loss contests, along with the standard fare of doctor, lawyer, cop, and firefighter shows, is still the medium for the masses. Then there's basic cable's menu of intellectual junk food, featuring the lunatic ravings of overindulged housewives, and other evolutionary throwbacks.

Intellectually, we're on a long, slow descent from the literati to the Twitterverse. Instead of allowing our brain farts to escape undetected into the atmosphere, we broadcast them in 140-character sound bites. Then, in some kind of coprophagic quip orgy, we retweet the tweets, and then retweet the retweets, collectively dining out on the slop of our own cleverness.

Despite a seemingly never-ending string of mass homicides, we continue to arm ourselves into the highest murder rate in the world. We think our status as stewards of the planet gives us the right to foul the planet itself. Shitting one's pants is considered a sign of immaturity. What civilized person shits his own house? And if it's true that you are what you eat, then we're a herd of overfed slobs who consume mass quantities of fatty, over-salted, high-calorie processed garbage. Then we stare in the mirror, baffled at the sight of our expanding waistlines, thinking this sudden, inexplicable obesity can be cured by a miracle diet, power cleanse, or appearance on a weight loss reality show. America: pockets of intelligence in a large pair of fat pants.

And at the root of our stupidity on issues from guns to education to gay marriage is our bone deep ignorance when it comes to religion. America is being held hostage by the Christian evangelical right. Repressive attitudes toward sex, women, homosexuality, and contraception, as well as superstition-based notions of life and death, have infected the culture, our educational system, and our government. People calling themselves Christians slam the brakes on social progress, grounding their self-righteousness in a literal interpretation of a book written thousands of years ago by people living halfway around the world. It's as if there's a Monkey Trial being waged over every aspect of modern life.

Our juvenile understanding of religion has also shackled us with a series of false arguments, the most idiotic being the alleged debate between evolution and creationism, grounded in the faulty assumption that every word in the Bible must be literally true, or it all falls apart. Religion as zero sum game.

In February 2014 there was a debate, moderated by CNN's Tom Foreman, between Bill Nye, the bow-tied science guy, and Ken Ham, creator and proprietor of the Creation Museum in Kentucky. The subject: God's existence. Frankly, they could've staged the debate between a hamster and an ashtray and it would've carried as much intellectual weight. Not that Mr. Nye doesn't seem like an intelligent science guy. And he makes the case for evolution as well as any adult can, though it's like trying to explain thermodynamics to a cat. But the real crime was that science was granted equal intellectual footing with Biblical superstition, moderated and thereby tacitly endorsed by a reporter from a major news outlet. The event was live-streamed by 750,000 computers, and became a fund-raising tool for Ham, helping him pay for his most-recent museum addition: a $73 million, 510-foot reconstruction of Noah's Ark. These days, media conglomerates bend over backwards to avoid offending religion, even religion at its most idiotic.

Now, you may note that HBO aired *Going Clear: Scientology and the Prison of Belief*. And it was brilliant, as well as long overdue. But the fact that Scientology is referred to in the media as a "controversial religion" is indicative of how little they, and we understand the subject. Scientology is not a religion. It never has been. It's a business that operates like a cult in the guise of a religion.

We assume Orwell's *1984* dystopian nightmare can't happen here, yet we've been narcotized into a more ominous Orwellian somnambulism. We're inebriated on our own mythology, priapic at our military supremacy, and malleable via our ionic imagery, whether it's Jesus or the flag. Jacked up on Adderall, Red Bull and patriotism, we only unite in war, tragedy and the Super Bowl. We've become style over substance, image over reality, propaganda over truth and symbol over meaning. We claim to value education, yet mistrust intelligence. Immune to facts, frightened of change, we think magically; magic potions that will heal us, magic diets that will shrink us, and magic beliefs that will save us. And we think all this behavior has been blessed by a big daddy in the sky who lovingly placed us here for profit, guns, and heterosexual marriage. Perhaps evolution is a myth, in that we seem to be devolving.

The Roman Empire collapsed due to war, overexpansion and rampant corruption. The British Empire dissolved due to cultural arrogance and imperialistic hubris. Sadly, as we devolve from Democracy to Idiocracy, America may become the first world power to crumble under the weight of its own stupidity.

CHAPTER TWO

DUMBF☰CK BELIEFS

"The fact that an opinion has been widely held is no evidence whatever that it is not utterly absurd."
Bertrand Russell

Americans worship the image of the tough-minded iconoclast; yet, when it comes to our basic assumptions about life, we don't think, we believe. And at the core of our national mindset – a cocktail of ignorance and philosophical relativism -- is our belief in belief, along with the assumption that having the right to our beliefs renders all beliefs equally valid.

We love our beliefs. We'll shove them down your throat whether you want to hear them or not. We stick them on T-shirts and bumper stickers; we even tattoo our bodies just to make sure that anyone who gets within spitting or screwing distance will instantly know where we stand. "This is what I believe" has become the rallying cry of the American idiot, despite the fact that beliefs, like opinions, are what stupid people have because they don't know, are too lazy to look for, or are too dumb to understand all the facts.

One in three Americans doesn't believe in evolution. Despite the fact that 99% of the world's scientists agree that climate change is real, and that we are in imminent danger of reaching a tipping point, a GOP Science Committee member can state, "Global warming is a total fraud," and the media gives him a pass. Then there's Trump's, "This global warming bullshit has got to stop. Our planet is freezing…" And for an argument that blends science denial and Biblical superstition in a delightful shithead sundae, there's Erick Erickson's, "The difference between people who believe in the second coming of Jesus and those who believe in global warming is that Jesus will return." One could teach a graduate seminar on all the boneheaded assumptions festering in that one statement.

But, it's not just ordinary nonsense like evolution being a theory, or the science being out on climate change. These are just stall tactics from people clinging to Biblical superstition, or stonewalling government regulations to protect their financial interests. There is a deeper, more fundamental ignorance about life in general, and our lives in particular, embedded in the American psyche. First off, we don't even know where we are.

OUR THINKING IS GEOCENTRIC

"Man is a little germ that lives on an unimportant rock ball that revolves about an insignificant star on the outer edges of one of the smaller galaxies."
Alan Watts

0.000000000000000000000000000000000000000000000000000003%. That's the size of the Earth in relation to the observable universe. We are a minor spec of dust, in a minor galaxy; in a universe that is so vast it would take an object travelling at the speed of light – 186,000 miles per second – 100,000 years to traverse it.

To get a sense of our cosmic insignificance, go on YouTube and search "how big is the Earth compared to the universe." You'll find a 3:44 video set to the Fourth Movement of Beethoven's Ninth Symphony that strikingly demonstrates how relatively tiny we are, compared to what is. Or, to get a feel for it, take out a saltshaker. Sprinkle some salt on the table. Spread it out. Now separate one grain to the side. That single grain of salt is the Earth. The state you live in is the universe.

We are a tiny blip in one of an estimated 125 billion galaxies, the result of an event dating back over 14 billion years, resulting in a confluence of energy, gasses and objects exploding and crashing into each other, only to give rise over time to a planet that could sustain carbon-based life. Whether that was a singular phenomenon or one of many is another matter, but the fact that our existence is the result of random events is too much for most people to wrap their minds around.

We just can't process the fact that we didn't have to be. It's like former Texas Governor Ann Richards' comment about George W. Bush: "He found himself standing on third base and assumed he hit a triple." Similarly, we find ourselves alive on Earth and assume we had to be here, as opposed to accepting the fact that we're the universe's happy accident, and that we're not here forever. We're in process, on a continuum, one that will eventually run its course and die. Our sun will burn for another 5 billion years and then flame out, taking the Earth with it. (You can read about these and other fun facts in a book entitled *1000 Questions and Answers,* published by *Discovery Kids.* It would make a wonderful Christmas gift for your favorite child, or your favorite creationist.)

Yet, despite all this nasty science, we still think the Earth was deliberately and lovingly placed here by a benevolent sky daddy who is personally concerned with the lives and afterlives of each and every one of us. That would be like you focusing on the hopes and dreams of a single cell in your body.

We also think we're so cosmically fabulous that aliens would travel millions of light years just for the privilege of checking us out. Given the mess we've made of the planet, and the misery we continue to inflict on each other, why would any life form capable of intergalactic travel visit this place, either to explore it, conquer it or, as in much of our popular fiction, take up residence in suburban neighborhoods and masquerade as Earth people? Contrary to the old SNL sketch, the Coneheads aren't aliens. The Coneheads are us.

OUR THINKING IS ANTHROCENTRIC

*"What a piece of work is a man! How noble
in reason, how infinite in faculty! In form and
moving how express and admirable. In action
how like an angel. In apprehension how like a god.
The beauty of the world. The paragon of animals.
And, yet to me, what is this quintessence of dust?"*
William Shakespeare

Despite being one of 8.7 million species existing on earth, we think the joint was created just for us. Laughable, when you consider that *homo sapiens* have only been around for about 200,000 years. At present, there are roughly 7 billion people on Earth, in 196 different countries, many of whom are actively engaged in the uniquely human activity of trying to wipe each other out.

Most creatures kill for food. We don't all kill for greed, money, land, jealousy, oil, power, ego, or God. Only man has figured that out. In the last century alone we've slaughtered some 108 million people, and 150 million to 1 billion throughout human history. Yet, we still refer to what we've got going on here as "civilization."

And that's just what we've done to each other. Look what we've done to the planet. Man took one look at paradise and decided what it needed was to be paved, mined, drilled, deforested, bombed, polluted, fracked and fouled to within an inch of its life.

Sure, we've dominated our world -- built roads, bridges, and skyscrapers. We drive cars, fly planes; we've molded the planet for our comfort and convenience, while categorizing every other living thing into pets to be domesticated, food to be eaten, or pests to be eliminated. The truth is, if every single human were wiped off the Earth tomorrow, in a hundred years the planet would probably revert to something resembling the mythical Garden of Eden -- pre-man, woman, snake, and apple.

Thinking of Hamlet's "what a piece of work is man" speech, it's true that we're the paragon of animals. Yet, we're also a "real piece of work" in the New Yorkese sense of being greedy, selfish, stupid, violent, and totally clueless.

OUR THINKING IS AMERICENTRIC

*"God bless America,
land that I love. Stand beside her,
and guide her, through the night
with the light from above..."*
Irving Berlin

We like to think that baseball is our national pastime. It's not. Even deeper than our profound love of baseball is the height of Tantric ecstasy we reach by blowing smoke up our own asses. First we devise the notion that this spec of cosmic gas and elements is the universe's Disneyland. Then we further display our arrogance by declaring that this particular country on this spec of dust is beloved by some imaginary creator. We're so engorged on national pride that we stop baseball games in the 7th inning just to sing a self-aggrandizing dirge celebrating how much the man in the sky loves us. We well up at songs, waving flags, and jets flying overhead spewing out red, white and blue smoke in a proud demonstration of patriotic flatulence. We get aroused over symbols but are too lazy or stupid to ponder the concepts they represent.

Don't get me wrong. I love baseball. I also love apple pie. And my first car was a Chevy. That's the all-American trifecta. But God Bless America? Really? That kind of arrogance not only takes some major self-delusion but also one cosmic set of balls. Yet, if you're at a game, you'd damn well better stand up and sing or you'll catch some patriotic hell from your fellow sports fans.

At the 2015 White House Correspondents Dinner, a *Washington Post* gossip columnist was spotted texting during the national anthem, and the media, along with many in the public, lost their collective minds. In 2011, when Tony Bennett made a comment about our culpability in 9/11, he was harshly criticized. Of course, the notion that the history of our Middle East foreign policy might have been even a contributing factor in creating the mindset that lead to our being attacked is anathema to most Americans. To paraphrase Santayana, it's not that we cannot remember the mistakes of the past, it's that we refuse to admit we ever made any. Much easier to adopt the evil empire approach, and explain world events as a Manichean struggle between good and evil. And then bomb evil out of existence.

As I sit on a plane on July 4th, a big guy comes walking down the aisle, wearing a tight, black T-shirt, with a graphic of a soldier holding a rifle. The caption below reads, "Back to Back World War Champs!" 17 million people died in World War I. 60 million were killed in World War II, almost 3% of the population, yet we can reduce that unfathomable carnage to the level of a baseball stat. We're not only drunk on watered down beer, but on our superiority as Americans, simply because we're Americans.

OUR THINKING IS EGOCENTRIC

*"All through the day
I me mine, I me mine, I me mine.
All through the night
I me mine, I me mine,
I me mine."*
George Harrison

To date, some 108 billion people have lived and died on Earth. Yet, we still think our individual lives are so fabulous that we celebrate them daily on social media. Socrates said the unexamined life is not worth living. Not anymore. It's the un-promoted life that's not worth living. Know thyself has morphed into flaunt thyself. Once upon a time, fame was tangentially related to talent, hard work, and accomplishment. Now the metric for evaluating a life is who's got more Facebook friends, Twitter, or Instagram followers.

We're so desperate to document our every living moment that we walk around with selfie sticks. In a sane society, the Taste Police would not only be empowered to confiscate them, but to beat the user about the face and head for the crime of felony narcissism. And similar street justice would be meted out for the celebrity selfie, the only purpose of which is to show that, for a fleeting moment in time, you were fame-adjacent.

We also think our precious little personalities are so etched in cosmic stone that our deaths couldn't possibly mark their end. That there's a special place we all go after we die: a magical, Jesus-themed park and sky mall that's divided into families and neighborhoods. And it's restricted. We don't bestow afterlife entrance on any other life form. We squash bugs, run over squirrels, shoot birds out of the sky, murder animals and eat them without a second thought for their immortal souls. Yet, somehow, we've decided that not only do we have souls, but that ours are eternal.

These unreflectively held assumptions about life in general and our own lives in particular are passed down through the generations and absorbed by the culture – by some as folklore, by others as fact. We'll gulp down colored juice concoctions to cleanse the toxins from our bodies; unfortunately, there's no mental colonic to flush out the effluence that's polluted our minds.

Our individual lives are fleeting blips on a radar screen, waves rolling in off the ocean. We're basically bags of meat with a backstory. There is nothing super fabulous or eternal about being Earth-dwellers, Americans, or humans; but try selling that idea to the average God-fearin', freedom-lovin', beer-swillin' patriot and see if he doesn't punch you out for being some kind of danged socialist. Because in America, we beat the hell out of ideas we don't like. That's called freedom.

CHAPTER THREE

DUMBF CK FREEDOM

ATLAS SHARTED

*"People demand freedom of speech
as a compensation for the freedom
of thought, which they seldom use."*
Soren Kierkegaard

We love our freedom. We're free to think, say, or write anything without fear of the Thought Police, or the actual police busting down the door and dragging us off for some political re-education and/or torture and/or death. And considering the misery humans have inflicted on each other over the millennia, and continue to inflict, it is something to treasure.

And we treasure the hell out of it. Every July 4th we get all gooey at the sight of grinning, teenage majorettes in sequined bathing suits leading a parade down Main Street. We cheer when they throw a sparkly stick in the air and catch it. We remove our hats and applaud as the veterans march or wheel behind, flashing their dignified salutes. And, of course, there's the adorable moppet standing on the curb, waving his tiny flag, having no clue what he's doing there beyond the fact that he's been told he gets ice cream. And at the end of the day we commemorate "the rockets red glare, the bombs bursting in air" by blasting the shit out of the sky and inducing heart attacks in any bird within a 5-mile radius.

I guess that's why July 4th is the most dangerous holiday of the year. In 2014, the National Safety Council estimated 385 Independence Day deaths and 41,200 injuries, including car crashes, swimming accidents, boating accidents, barbecue burns, and fireworks explosions, with alcohol playing a major factor. There are 20,000 trips to the ER every July 4th. Check out some recent headlines:

*Washington State Boater Missing After
Boozy July 4th Crash*

North Carolina Girl, 17, Killed by Alleged Drunk Boater

*New York Giants Defensive End
Blows Off Fingers in July 4th Fireworks Accident*

Fargo Man Beheaded by Fourth of July Fireworks

Man Blows Off Hand in July 4th Accident

*Boat Propeller Severs Man's Leg
in July 4th Boating Accident*

*Woman Loses Foot at Illegal
July 4th Fireworks Accident*

*Dozens Hurt in July 4th Fireworks
Accident in Simi Valley*

*July 4th Fireworks Accident Injuries 90
in New Hampshire*

*Maine Man Dies After Launching
Fireworks From Top of His Head*

Fireworks Accident Claims Man's Testicles

Man Blows off Part of His Genitals with Fireworks

Somehow we got from "don't fire until you see the whites of their eyes!" to "somebody find my nuts and call an ambulance!" Maybe, subconsciously, it's a bonding ritual with the pain the troops went through, like the Shi'a Muslim *Day of Ashura,* when they cut themselves to commemorate those who died at the 680 A.D. Battle of Karbala. They lash themselves with swords and chains. We blow our nuts off. Maybe it could be a road to discovering some kind of cross-cultural commonality. Maybe not. We're not that deep. We just like blowing shit up, pounding beers, and eating barbecue for freedom.

Again, don't get me wrong: I love July 4th. Picnics. Hot dogs. And who doesn't love fireworks. One of my fondest memories of the holiday is from the summer after my sophomore year of college. My girlfriend and I got a ride to Eisenhower Park on Long Island. We had a little picnic. Then, in preparation for the fireworks, we dropped acid. As dusk fell and the fireworks started, we gawked and gaped right along with the crowd. Each colorful blast put smiles on everyone's faces. And we all lit up at the explosive finale, leaving that distinct smell of gunpowder wafting in the air. Then the families packed up their coolers and kids, and split, while we sat on our blanket still gazing at the sky. I'm guessing they didn't see what we saw. I'm also guessing this wasn't what Eisenhower had in mind when they named a park after him.

Yet, aside from hot dogs, fireworks, parades, and physical dismemberment, if you ask the average American what the holiday is about, the knee-jerk response would be "freedom." But for all our bragging, parading, weeping, saluting, and genital self-mutilation for freedom, we really don't understand the concept. In fact, our national dialogue on the subject is grounded in two big lies.

THE FIRST BIG LIE
FREEDOM = LICENSE

In April 2015, Rand Paul appeared before a partisan crowd in his hometown of Louisville, Kentucky to announce his run for the presidency. This came as no surprise, as in 2014 he came out with the obligatory "I'm running for president" book, entitled: *Taking a Stand! Moving Beyond Partisan Politics to Unite America.* The title was meant to portray him as a reasonable guy, and not some anti-government whack job. It was also an attempt to correct any misapprehensions people may have gotten from his first book: *Government Bullies: How Everyday Americans are Being Harassed, Abused and Imprisoned by the Feds.* He barnstormed the country for years, just like his daddy did when he unsuccessfully ran for president in 1988, 2008, and 2012. Ron Paul – a twangy, mini-Texan with an Ayn Rand fixation so deep he named his son after her.

(Ayn Rand was the godmother of laissez faire capitalism, the Virgin Mary of Libertarianism. She died in 1982. She spent her life attempting to turn selfishness into a religion so that people could claim their greed was grounded in the nature of man. Her heinous ideas and crappy books have given politicians philosophical cover to promote their "greed is good" agenda for decades. Too rough? Go on YouTube and check out her smug, 1959 interview with Mike Wallace, and see if you don't have the urge to dig her up and kick her in the teeth.)

For a nanosecond, Ron Paul was a refreshing new voice on the American political scene, a relief from the typical Romneybot haircut hovering over a suit. If you listened to Paul for five minutes, he seemed to make sense, especially with his opposition to the Iraq War. Unfortunately, if you listened for another five minutes, you realized he was just another Libertarian lunatic screeching about the jackbooted government thugs who are coming to take our freedom.

With Rand Paul it was different; you didn't even get the first five minutes. In almost childlike responses to media questions, a cocky smirk crept across his lips as he wrapped the entirety of his message in the simple declaration, "I'm for freedom," admittedly, a courageous stance for an American politician. Paul even tried to make the case that declaring universal health care a fundamental human right would be the equivalent of military conscription. He claimed that, as a licensed ophthalmologist, he could be forced to treat a patient against his will.

Right. So, one Sunday morning Rand's in the kitchen making flapjacks for the kids, when suddenly the door is kicked open by a gang of government stormtroopers who drag him outside, throw him in the trunk of a car, and spirit him away to a remote black site where he's forced to treat some immigrant's astigmatism. Yeah, that could happen. That's some solid, presidential thinking.

But for all his pandering, and even his "hey, I'm just a regular guy" TV appearances, Rand has had as much success running for the presidency as his father did; i.e., none. But how is it he got any traction at all? It's because we don't understand the concept of freedom.

Thanks to the Rand Pauls and Paul Ryans of the world, a system of government based on the rights of the individual has morphed into a Randian deification of the individual. The Preamble to the Constitution begins with "We, the people" not "I, the person." It's a political document grounded in the rights of man, and inspired by Athenian democracy, the Magna Carta, the English Bill of Rights, and the Mayflower Compact.

Paul's version of freedom is based on the simplistic notion that what's great about America is that we can all just do whatever we want without government interference. Essentially, "you're not the boss of me." And whether it's spoken by a child to a parent, or by a citizen to a government, the juvenile mindset is the same. It confuses freedom with license. It also confuses "freedom from," as in not being subjected to the tyranny of a repressive monarchy or dictatorship, with "freedom to," as in being free to carry an AR-15 into a Chipotle.

Our political system is based on the rights of the individual in society, not the sanctification of the individual as some autonomous entity. Freedom is a group experience, grounded in the social contract. That's why we call it "living in a free society." Declaring everyone free is not the same as declaring life a free-for-all. Speed limits, stops signs, and traffic lights aren't limits on our freedom to drive as fast as we want. They're rules for the common good. Prosecutors in a courtroom are there to represent the people, not to pursue some private agenda.

Freedom is something we experience individually, and share collectively. Governments exist to safeguard it. Unfortunately, this idea has all but evaporated from the American conversation. Trying to grasp the yin/yang of individual desire and group responsibility seems to create a cognitive dissonance that sends most Americans running for a beer to make the thinking stop. It's much sexier to strap on your six guns and wade into the public square doing your best Yosemite Sam impression.

In the early '80s, Thatcherism took root in England, coinciding with the election of Ronald Reagan, the right's political Jesus, and Margaret Thatcher's spiritual fuck buddy. Reagan took a shot at the presidency in 1968 and 1976, before hitting the right time to sell his Gipper-esque "shining city on a hill" rap to a public tired of inflation, and feeling emasculated by Jimmy Carter's inability to free the Iran hostages.

(The Reagan hagiography still lives today, despite the fact that he was a second-rate actor who, according to the 1986 book *Dark Victory: Ronald Reagan, MCA and the Mob*, sold out his union [SAG] during a negotiation, was an FBI informant during the McCarthy era blacklists, and had the beginnings of Alzheimer's while in office, but apparently forgot to mention it which, I guess, could be chalked up to his having Alzheimer's.)

At any rate, at that time the Iron Lady said:

> *"There is no such thing [as society].*
> *There are individual men and women*
> *and there are families and no government*
> *can do anything except through people*
> *and people look to themselves first…"*

Not exactly the kind of enlightened statement one would expect from the leader of a democratic world power. Despite masquerading as a call for self-reliance, it was essentially another Randian apologetic for selfishness and screwing the poor. Self interest *uber alles*.

But even on the theoretical level, the argument doesn't hold up. Those who claim there's no society want to limit the role of the federal government because of the restrictions it places on an individual. This means putting more power in the hands of the states; an idea at the core of the Republican political agenda, despite our ugly history with states rights. But there's nothing inherently less autocratic or bureaucratic about state government than the fed; therefore, you need to hand power down to the cities. Same problem. Then it's down to towns and neighborhoods. Still the same problem. You're in an argument of infinite regression because, at every step, you have some larger body making rules for and "limiting the freedom" of individuals. Might as well make each household an autonomous governing body. Yet, even then, the family breaks down to a state of nature, and dinnertime becomes a firefight over who gets the last meatball.

This argument came up more recently with a stance backed by New Jersey Governor and 2016 presidential aspirant Chris Christie. Commenting on the so-called anti-vaxxer movement, Christie stated, "It's about choice." Wrong. How about this time, Governor, as you're so fond of telling reporters, you sit down, shut up, and stop saying stupid things. Vaccinating your kids isn't about parental choice. It's about verifiable science, public health, and social responsibility, particularly considering the fact that every school classroom I've ever visited was a greasy, grimy Petri Dish of germs and airborne snot. Letting your unvaxxed spawn run amok in that hamster cage is not an expression of your freedom. It's an expression of you being a selfish dick. Or dickette. And will result in creating a new generation of Typhoid Megans and Dylans.

The Declaration of Independence and Constitution are social and political documents. The federalism/states rights argument goes back to the beginning of our democracy. Resistance to a strong fed was a safeguard against it amassing too much power -- a hangover from being ruled by a king. However, at times, the government has had to serve as the conscience of the nation and use its power on behalf of what was morally right, or economically necessary, whether that meant sending troops to a Southern university to ensure that black students could attend class, bailing out a flooded city, or a tanking economy.

As with most things in life, it's about striking a balance between self-interest and social responsibility. Too much Groupthink, you get totalitarianism. Too much individualism, you get *Lord of the Flies*. We still place value on morality in this country. And most theories of morality are predicated on the good of the many. Whether it's Mill's "greatest good for the greatest number," or Kant's Categorical Imperative: "Act only according to that maxim by which you can at the same time will that it should become a universal law." Even Mr. Spock's poignant self-sacrifice at the end of *Star Trek II: The Wrath of Khan* was marked by his declaration that "the needs of the many outweigh the needs of the few. Or the one." We need each other to survive, and thrive. Free-for-all isn't liberty. It's anarchy.

But if you still insist there's no society, then you'd better stockpile more guns, ammo, and Spaghettios because eventually there'll be 325 million of your fellow Americans coming to take your shit. And when you're locked inside your personal fortress, weapon at the ready, scanning your property line for the walking dead, stop and reflect on whether this is the best way to live.

It's time to elevate the conversation, particularly when it comes to a concept as fundamental to our system of government as freedom. When the Joanie Ernsts of the world start squawking about needing a gun to protect herself from the day the government comes to take her freedom, someone with a public voice has to call her out, instead of, you know, electing her to Congress.

Despite the scare tactics politicians use to freak out Americans into arming themselves against the onslaught of the federal government, it's just not going to happen. The government's not deploying the army to your town to snatch your freedom. Arming yourself to the teeth in preparation for this mythical Alamo doesn't make you a "don't tread on me" patriot. It makes you a paranoid, heavily armed schmuck.

If you really want to understand the loss of freedom, drop the gun, tune out the bellicose ravings of your favorite corpulent shock jock, and listen to the voices of those who have lived their lives under oppression. People who actually had their freedom taken away, or never even had it in the first place.

*"For to be free is not merely to cast off
one's chains, but to live in a way,
that respects and enhances the freedom of others."*
Nelson Mandela
Imprisoned for 27 years

*"I would like to be remembered
as a person who wanted to be free…
so that other people would also be free."*
Rosa Parks

*"Human beings want to be free and however long
they may agree to stay locked up, to stay oppressed,
there will come a time when they say 'That's it.'
Suddenly, they find themselves doing something
that they never would have thought they would be doing,
simply because of the human instinct that
makes them turn their face towards freedom."*
Aung San Suu Kyi
15 years under house arrest

*"You only have power over people so long as you don't
take everything away from them. But when
you've robbed a man of everything he's no longer
in your power. He's free."*
Aleksandr Solzhenitsyn
Expelled from the Soviet Union for 20 years

*"Hatred is corrosive of a person's wisdom and
conscience; the mentality of enmity can poison
a nation's spirit, instigate brutal life and death
struggles, destroy a society's tolerance and humanity,
and block a nation's progress to freedom and democracy."*
Liu Xiaobo
Incarcerated

*"Freedom is never voluntarily given by the oppressor;
it must be demanded by the oppressed."*
Dr. Martin Luther King, Jr.
Murdered

*"Nobody can give you freedom.
Nobody can give you equality
or justice, or anything. If you're a

man, you just take it."
Malcolm X
Murdered

*"Intellectual freedom is essential – freedom
to obtain and distribute information,
freedom for open-minded and
unfearing debate and freedom from
pressure by officialdom and prejudices.
Such freedom of thought is the only
guarantee against an infection of people
by mass myths, which, in the hands of
treacherous hypocrites and
demagogues, can be transformed
into bloody dictatorship."*
Andrei Sakharov
Lived in exile for 6 years

*"Human rights are universal and indivisible.
Human freedom is also indivisible: if it is
denied to anyone in the world, it is
therefore denied, indirectly, to all people.
This is why we cannot remain silent in the
face of evil or violence;
silence merely encourages them."*
Vaclav Havel
Imprisoned for 4 years

*"We hold our heads high, despite
the price we have paid,
because freedom is priceless."*
Lech Walesa
Imprisoned for 11 months

"The price of freedom is eternal vigilance."
Archbishop Desmond Tutu

*"Human beings, indeed all sentient beings,
have the right to pursue happiness and live
in peace and freedom."*
Dalai Lama
In exile for 57 years

"I lived in countries that had no democracy…

so I don't find myself in the same luxury
you do. You grew up in freedom,
and you can spit on freedom because
you don't know what it is not to have freedom."
Ayaan Hirsi Ali
Lives under death threats

"What is freedom of expression?
Without the freedom to offend, it ceases to exist."
Salman Rushdie
Lives under death threats

"I believe I have the right to live
my life the way I want."
Malala Yousafzai
Shot

"The weapon of the word is stronger
than bullets, because authorities will profit
from a battle of weapons."
Ayatollah Nimr al-Nimr
Executed

THE SECOND BIG LIE
FREEDOM = LAISSEZ FAIRE CAPITALISM

"Them that's got shall have
Them that's not shall lose
So, the Bible said, and it still is news
Mama have have, Papa may have
But God bless the child that's got his own..."
Billie Holiday

Back in 2010, Bill O'Reilly said something interesting on *Real Time with Bill Maher*. No, really, he did. Toward the end of their discussion about the Bush tax cuts and whether the wealthy could withstand a 3% bump without committing mass suicide and sending the country into an economic death spiral, O'Reilly commented: "...the philosophy is that income redistribution isn't in the Constitution. It wasn't how the country was set up. This is a capitalistic society."

Granted, O'Reilly has made some ignorant, even hateful comments in the past, but compared to the gaggle of special needs adults who populate Murdochia, he's Aristotle. But that comment nagged at me for a while until I figured out why. What he said was dead wrong. Dead wrong. And it's a dead wrongness that is at the root of our misunderstanding of the concept of freedom. It's also an insidious lie trotted out by the right to conflate democratic freedom with capitalistic license. (Ayn Rand, you deranged, arrogant, heartless, selfish bitch! Shut up and stay dead!)

Here's the wrong part: we don't live in a capitalistic society. We <u>work</u> in a capitalist <u>system</u>. We <u>live</u> in a democratic <u>society</u>. And just to make sure, I checked what the Preamble to the Constitution had to say about capitalism, as I seemed to remember it being more of a statement of basic human rights than an economic manifesto. Here is what it says about capitalism: nothing. It says:

> *"We the People of the United States in Order to form a more perfect Union, establish Justice, insure domestic Tranquility, provide for the common defence, promote the general Welfare and secure the Blessings of Liberty to ourselves and for Posterity do ordain and establish this Constitution for the United States of America."*

Note the language: "we," "us," "union," "general welfare." No "I" statements, or money statements. Then I checked the history of capitalism. According to a book entitled *A Short History of Capitalism*:

> *"...the American economy became predominantly*
> *capitalist only by 1900. The earlier years*
> *fall into three periods. The first, from 1600 to 1790,*
> *is characterized by handicraft-subsistence*
> *production alongside elements of a*

> *semi-capitalist economy stemming from commercial production of tobacco. The most commercialized sectors of the economy were predominantly staffed by enslaved and semi-enslaved workers..."*

Wouldn't be too eager to brag about the whole slavery part. It continues:

> *"...During the second period, 1790-1865, several industries became organized along capitalist lines... In the third period, 1865-1920 ... industry and agriculture become subject to capitalist forces."*

So, no capitalism around the time of the Constitution. Not that I'm knocking capitalism. I like capitalism. Abuses aside, it works because it places value on an individual's drive to work hard and enjoy the benefits of economic success. That's why communism imploded. You can't stifle the individual human spirit. When you try, people tend to rebel, and eventually you find yourself having to seize power to keep them in check. You know, for the good of the people. Not exactly the dictatorship of the proletariat. More like the dictatorship of the dictatorship. Not to mention the rampant corruption that tends to exist among those at the top. Communism may seem equitable on paper. It just doesn't work when you attach actual human beings.

On the other hand, absolute power corrupts absolutely. And that includes absolute economic power. Karl Marx wrote in 19th century England in reaction to the abuses of capitalism during the Industrial Revolution. If workers were treated fairly under capitalism, communism would have never arisen. Nor would there have been a need for unions.

Disenfranchised people eventually reach a level of desperation and hopelessness, echoed in a Kris Kristofferson song: "Freedom's just another worth for nothing left to lose." The American, French, and Russian revolutions are testaments to that. The U.S. labor movement didn't arise spontaneously, or because workers are just greedy bastards who enjoy screwing management. And management didn't exactly welcome their formation. From the Pinkertons hired by Henry Ford to bust up strikes, to Reagan firing the air traffic controllers, to Scott Walker's Koch Brothers-fueled efforts in Wisconsin, the history of union busting is evidence of their necessity.

That's why Republicans criticize any law designed to regulate corporations as an "attack on freedom." But that's freedom perverted into a sanctification of greed. It's a time-tested line of bullshit that's become embedded in Republican rhetoric. At times it seems that what they're really after is the state-sponsored capitalism in China. In terms of human rights and freedom of expression, it's a communist nightmare. In terms of business operating without limits, and with government complicity, it's an anarcho-capitalist's wet dream.

But just as communism fails because it negates the individual, capitalism risks crumbling when it denies our communal experience. We've bought into the false notion that our rugged American individualism is something that exists in spite of other people, not because of them. During the 2012 election, President Obama tried to make the subtle point that we rely on one another for our success, but due to the unfortunately phrased "you didn't build that" inadvertently handed Republicans a talking point. Despite taking great pains to make the case that underlying individual achievement is a strategic use of our communal resources, it was a subtlety lost on an unthinking electorate.

The fact is we work for ourselves, and we work for each other. Think of a simple thing you do every day, like driving to work. You feel pretty independent behind the wheel; AC blasting, music cranking, captain of the ship, master of your domain. But consider this: Did you make the car? Design the car? Build the car? Transport it to the dealer? Sell it? Did you drill for the oil and refine it into gasoline? Transport it to the gas station? Open the gas station and run the business? Did you build the roads you're driving on? Design the system of traffic lights and install them? Do you patrol the streets to make sure no one drives like a maniac or shoots anyone going 45 in the fast lane? Did you launch the satellites that send directions to your GPS? Did you create the music you're listening to? Brew and sell the coffee you're drinking? Jump off the roof from the stress of working in the Chinese factory that built the iPhone you're not supposed to be texting on?

There's an invisible net of other people's work in most every moment of our lives. How those individual jobs are rewarded is indicative of our values. The musician who recorded the song on the radio is probably better off than the factory worker who installed the bumpers on your car. Of course, some people might say, "I made my money with my hard work, and I deserve my rewards, so screw everybody else. Why should it matter to me how they live?" And that's fine. Be a selfish asshole. Just don't try to fob it off as a legitimate social and political philosophy.

But while you're doing that, you might want to consider what kind of world you'll be living in when millions of your fellow Americans have to struggle every day just to get by. That's assuming they can get by. You may live in a beautiful house and drive an expensive car, but will the desperate people around you respect them? How many homeless people will you drive by getting off the freeway? How many will hit you up for change while you're shopping in the mall? How many waiters will spit in your food? Even if Jesus was wrong and the wealthy inherit the Earth, what shape will it be in when they get it?

It's interesting that the party that rejects biological evolution seems to have no problem with economic evolution; survival of the richest. It's also interesting, and hypocritical, that many who wear their Christianity as a badge of honor have made it their business to gut every social program designed to help those less fortunate. Reagan's welfare queen lie still lives and breathes as "entitlements." The reasoning is that any assistance will just make people lazy and dependent. Maybe so; though, if the Rand Pauls and Paul Ryans really want to back up their play about cutting social programs because they dis-incentivize people from looking for work, they shouldn't puss out. Don't gut those programs. Just pass a law mandating the execution of anyone making less than fifty grand a year. Now that would be an incentive to get off your ass and find a job.

As with power, greed corrupts, and absolute greed corrupts absolutely. And there's no more poignant example of sociopathic greed run amok than Bernie Madoff, whose $50 billion Ponzi scheme came crashing down in 2008, decimating the savings and the lives of his investors.

Madoff's downfall was almost Shakespearean. Imprisoned for life. Wife dumps him. One son commits suicide. Another dies of cancer. Reviled to the point that his name has become synonymous with pure evil. Though I doubt this lead Madoff to any "come to Jesus" moment. My guess is that, to his dying day, his only regret will be that he got busted. That's why I would let him go and allow him to keep all the money he stole. I'll pause for the outrage, then explain.

I would let him live in his New York apartment with the billions he scammed, but with the proviso that everyone else agreed not to accept a dime from him in exchange for performing any services. No one would sell him food, or serve him in restaurants. No one would service his building. No water. No heat in the winter. No AC in summer. And no one would talk to him. Let him rot in his penthouse or roam the streets, a social pariah, starving to death, reduced to offering strangers a million bucks for a tuna sandwich. Maybe then he would come to the realization that our lives are connected.

At some point we have to dispense with the childish notions of freedom as license, or as unfettered capitalism. Individual effort takes place in society. We need each other to survive. You want to declare Christianity the national religion? Fine. Christianity is compassionate. You know, blessed are the meek, and all that. You want one? Accept the other. Just stop trying to square that circle with the prosperity gospel. I don't think Jesus said, "screw the meek." I definitely don't remember a passage in the Beatitudes about low corporate taxes. And I don't think the point of the Sermon on the Mount was that we should all just suck on the teats of our individual fortunes, treating others' misfortune as evidence of weakness, laziness, or moral failing. And if we can't smarten up enough to comprehend this simple concept, then maybe we need to re-think this whole American experiment. It's been 240 years since the Revolutionary War. Maybe it's time to give it up and go back home to England.

So, how about it, England, will you take us back? We'll behave this time. No more revolutions. We'll adopt the parliamentary system and take the universal health care. We'll make a fuss about the queen and totally lose our shit when some royals hook up, or squirt out a baby. "The heir and the spare! How delightful!" We'll stop flossing. We'll ditch football and go full-time soccer. We'll even call it football. We already know how to riot whether our team wins or loses, so we'll fit right in. We'll take English lessons and learn to speak proper. Properly. We'll drink the warm beer. We'll ditch our Hooters and Fridays restaurants and rename them Hounds and Frogs, or Dragons and Tampons, or whatever you call them. We'll even try that stuff you call food that's boiled animal guts in a pie, or the one where you turn a sheep inside-out.

Sure, we know you've got your own problems. But you've been around for over a thousand years. You're an adult; we're just a flailing, out-of-control child. We need help. Guidance. We've been given too much freedom so we just run amok, eating ice cream, watching violent cartoons, getting morbidly obese, blowing our nuts off, then having a tantrum at bedtime 'cause we're all hopped up on sugar. We're fat, sloppy, lazy and stupid. But we have tons of land, not all of it fracked, and good dentists. So, take us home. You can call us anything you like. *Southern Canada.* Or *New and Improved England! Now with 20% More Intelligence!* Please think about it. To show you we're serious, we'll even give up our guns. And you know how much we love our guns.

CHAPTER FOUR

DUMBF CK POWER

"Happiness is a warm gun."
The Beatles

I shot a gun once, and I liked it. It was a double-barrel .12 gauge shotgun. It was 1969 and I had tickets for Woodstock. Some friends and I planned to drive up with a high school shop teacher, who would ostensibly keep an eye on us. Then my parents informed me they'd booked a family cruise to the Caribbean. I protested. Stomped around. Had a proper teenage fit. It didn't fly. So, I ditched my hash pipe for shorts and flip-flops and cruised the islands.

My only solace was that my friends never made it, either. As Arlo Guthrie gleefully announced in the movie -- which I saw in New York the day it came out, for my vicarious Woodstock experience -- "The New York State Thruway's closed, man!" And it was. The traffic was backed up for miles. My friends ended up camping in the woods for a night. Then they turned around and went home.

So, I didn't miss out. Though years later it occurred to me: why would a single shop teacher escort a group of high school boys away on a trip? If I remember, he wasn't one of those hip guys who took a teaching job just to dodge the draft. He was some bald, hairy knuckle type. In hindsight, I may have been saved hours stuck in traffic, the disappointment of never making it to Woodstock, and some potentially weird moments in the woods with the shop teacher.

I did, however, get my quasi Woodstock experience years later at the 1973 Summer Jam at Watkins Glen, held at a racetrack in upstate New York, and attended by 600,000 people. Friends and I dropped acid the night before, then spent the day working on the roof of a house, laying asphalt shingles over tarpaper, in 90-degree heat. Then I hooked up with a girl I knew and we took off in her sky blue VW Bug. And by "took off" I mean crept, bumper-to-bumper. It took us 5 hours to drive 36 miles.

We finally got there, ran into some friends, and we all slept in a field. The next day we walked to the site and baked in the blistering sun for hours before seeing The Grateful Dead and The Band. Then the Allman Brothers came on, and we may have lasted until the intro to *Stormy Monday* before agreeing we were fried. So, we split. After spending an hour looking for the car, we were about to get in when a fat guy came out of his house barking something about "damn hippies." He was holding a shotgun, which was, I guess, the point of this nostalgic side-trip. Guns.

Anyway… Woodstock. That's when I fired a gun, skeet shooting off the deck of a cruise ship with my father. Ok, so it wasn't exactly a young Masai warrior venturing into the jungle for his first lion kill, but it was still a rite of passage for a suburban kid. I can still feel the powerful kick from the stock slamming into my shoulder. It may have been the summer of peace and love, but I have to confess I got a rush blasting clay dishes out of the sky.

So, I'm not anti-gun. Growing up I had a closetful of toy guns. My father brought home a Japanese rifle from his stint on a PT boat in the Pacific during WWII. Although the firing pin was removed, we would still take it out in the neighborhood and play war. We also blew up garbage cans with cherry bombs on July 4th. You know, to show our patriotism.

One summer we got the brilliant idea to get an empty Co2 cartridge, cut off the tip with a hacksaw, stuff it with match heads, with one match sticking out, and put the projectile at the bottom of a long tube tilted at a 45-degree angle. Then we lit the match, and the thing shot out like a rocket across several backyards. I remember thinking it was pretty ingenious for a bunch of brats to figure out how to build a homemade mortar. Despite many parents' adamantine stance against their kids playing with guns, let's be honest, people like to shoot shit.

I'm also not a vegetarian. Even as a sheltered suburbanite, I knew that meat wasn't something that started life wrapped in plastic. I knew the cows didn't jump off a cliff, despondent over a lost love. I knew the chickens didn't wring their own necks. And I was pretty sure the fish didn't commit suicide by jumping out of the ocean into waiting nets for the privilege of appearing in my tuna sandwich. Even now, the free-rangiest chicken ends up dead on my plate, despite the momentary illusion that he was out there running wild and living the good life. Not like those sorry bastards stuck in the coop. I get that there's a level of hypocrisy among carnivores who turn a blind eye to how the food got there. I also think it's willful ignorance to think that the cows we slaughter for our cheeseburgers don't feel pain and suffer. I think they do. No matter how they live, eventually they're cruelly and dispassionately murdered and carved up for steaks. I don't, however, think plants feel pain. That's just retarded.

I also have nothing against hunting. Though, personally, I don't think I could get Bambi's mom in my sights and pull the trigger. At my old house, a family of deer would jump the fence and stroll around, eating leaves off the trees. I knew they were skittish so I didn't approach them. I also didn't want Lyme Disease. So, I just stood there, observing nature up close, while appreciating the fact that we were living in some sort of harmony. I never thought, "Shit, if only I had a gun I could blow their Bambi heads off."

But if that's your thing, have at it. If you like venison, and share Native Americans' appreciation for the animal's sacrifice, then hunt. I know for some it's a father/son thing. Or a father/daughter thing. Hell, even if it's just a dick thing. If Ted Nugent wants to dress up in his soldier suit and run around the woods with a bow and arrow shooting bunny rabbits, who cares? Well, other than the rabbits. But if it keeps him in the woods and stops him from playing his crappy music or opening his ignorant mouth, then fine. Even if you're just a sadist who graduated from burning ants on the sidewalk to running around the woods with a high-powered rifle, given modern American life, I suppose it's better to kill a few forest creatures than people at the mall.

But here in the U.S., we're not all hunters. We're gun nuts. The U.S. has more guns per resident than any nation in the world: 325 million people, between 270 and 310 million guns. That's a Glock in every pot. Per capita, there are only two countries in the world more armed than we are: Serbia and Yemen.

With less than 5% of the world's population we have between 35-50% of the world's civilian-owned guns. You'd think that would make us the most dangerous place in the world. We're not. That distinction goes to Brazil with 34,678 gun deaths in a recent year, followed by Colombia, Mexico, and Venezuela. Then we came in with 9,146. Although in another year, we made it up to 10,728, a difference of 1,500 people. Not a big difference, unless of course you happen to be one of those 1,500 people.

So, we're not the world's deadliest place. Although if you factor in what we like to call the civilized world, in the year when there were 10,728 handgun deaths in the U.S., there were 48 in Japan, 8 in Great Britain, 34 in Switzerland, 52 in Canada, 58 in Israel, 21 in Sweden, and 42 in West Germany.

In the U.S., guns kill an average of 36 people every day. Guns kill more people than car accidents in 14 states. In a recent year, gun suicides outnumbered traffic deaths in Alaska, Washington, Oregon, Nevada and Utah. Utah, called the most depressed state in the country, has 275 firearm suicides a year. No alcohol, caffeine, or pre-marital sex? Yeah, I get that. According to a report from the Gun Violence Archive, by late 2015 we'd already racked up 49,771 gun incidents, resulting in 12,587 deaths and 25,474 injuries. We also had 317 mass shootings. And we still hadn't made it to Christmas.

Still, we accept the perverse argument that guns make us safer. A recent study by the Violence Policy Center found there were 258 justifiable homicides involving citizens using firearms in 2012, compared with 8,342 murders by gun. Another study revealed that right-to-carry laws have been linked to a rise in violent crimes. We have open carry laws in 44 of 50 states. In 2015, Texas passed an open carry law for those who have gun licenses, even allowing them to take their weapons into psychiatric hospitals. The state has 925,000 people with gun licenses. And it's really hot. And it's lousy with Texans. So, what could go wrong?

But it's not just gun culture. It's American culture and our national hard-on for violence, manifested in movies and video games. They stoke twisted revenge fantasies that play right into teenage angst, and the marginalized outsider's rage. Guns have become the misanthrope's language -- bullets the angry loner's vocabulary. We should hardly be surprised when some lunatic grabs his AR-15 and shoots up a schoolyard, mall, or movie theater. You know, so he'll be remembered. Because, for some, infamy is as close as they'll ever get to fame. And fame in modern American culture is the new currency. The "shitcoin," if you will.

It doesn't take a genius to figure it out. Stats don't lie. It's a very simple equation: more guns, more death. Take a minute to let it sink in: more guns, more death.

And that's just people committing murder so they'll feel better. We've also had our political assassinations. Lincoln, Garfield, McKinley, JFK. RFK, Martin Luther King, Malcolm X. Teddy Roosevelt was shot. Reagan was shot. George

Wallace was shot. Ford was shot at. Just because we have freedom of speech doesn't mean we won't take a shot at you if we don't like what you're saying.

And, of course, there's celebrity murder. On December 8, 1980, I was in my apartment on East 92nd Street in New York, when I turned on the news and learned that, right across town, John Lennon had been shot outside his apartment. Stunned, all I could do was stare at the TV, watching the people gathered outside the Dakota sing and hold up candles. I had no urge to hop in a cab and race crosstown to join them. I'm just not the candle-holding type.

But as a boomer with Beatles music in my DNA and Lennon songs in my head, every so often I stop and think about the music he might have created over the last 35 years. Then I think of that sad, twisted prick in prison and wish that every morning you could queue up outside his cell, and when he stuck his head out to get his breakfast, you could step up and punch him in the face. I'd wait in that line. But, I wouldn't shoot him, because violence doesn't solve anything.

Though not content with killing each other one at a time, we have our other national pastime: mass murder. In August 1966, an engineering student at the University of Texas, Austin, and a former U.S. Marine, flipped out and shot his wife and mother. Then he went to campus, climbed a bell tower, and killed 16 people, while wounding 32, before he was shot and killed by police.

In 1999, a couple of unloved teenagers strolled into Columbine High, armed with a Tec-9, a 9mm semi-automatic handgun, a sawed-off 12-gauge pump shotgun, and a 10-shot carbine rifle, along with a backup arsenal of knives and pipe bombs. The guns were obtained illegally. They fired 188 rounds, killing 13 people and wounding 24. They also committed suicide at the scene. (Just days after Columbine, former NRA celebrity spokesman, Charlton Heston, appeared at a gun rally in Denver, defiantly held a musket over his head and, grinning his cocky grin, uttered his stock phrase, "from my cold dead hands." Heston died in 2008. Just curious: has anyone dug him up to make sure they took the gun from his cold, dead hands?)

Still, at the time, Columbine felt like an aberration. Something that just didn't happen in American life. Oh, to be nostalgic for 20th century occasional mass murder. Since then we've had Virginia Tech, in 2007: 32 killed, 17 wounded, by a shooter armed with a 9mm Glock and a Walther p22 pistol he bought legally. Even with a history of mental illness.

Then there was Tucson, in 2011, where a gunman, later diagnosed as a paranoid schizophrenic, killed 6 and wounded 13, including Congresswoman Gabby Gifford, with a semi-automatic weapon he bought legally.

In 2012, there was the Aurora, Colorado movie theater shooting: 12 killed, 70 wounded.

And in the same year, in the one mass murder that should have galvanized the nation to demand that government act on the problem, a twisted little monster murdered his mother then went on a rampage at Sandy Hook Elementary school killing 20 children and 6 adults. And, still, Congress didn't move on any form of gun control, despite support from almost 90% of Americans.

As I write this on a smog-covered L.A. morning, today's news brought the story of a 21-year-old gunman in Charleston, South Carolina who sat in a black church, then just got up, screamed a bunch of racist bile, and killed 9 people. The shooter, a 9th grade dropout with two arrests, bought the gun for himself as a 21st birthday present.

After the shooting, a report surfaced, stating that police had previously stopped the suspect. A field review of his car turned up six 40-round AR-15 magazines in his trunk. He told police he'd wanted an AR-15, but just couldn't afford it. So, this twisted little shit was a just a fast food job away from killing more people, and starting the race war he'd been fantasizing about. Might actually be an excuse for not raising the minimum wage.

As of that shooting, I thought I was up to date on mass murder. Not quite. In July 2015, some maniac in Louisiana sat in a movie theater then suddenly opened fire with a .40-calibre semiautomatic pistol, killing 2 people, and wounding 9. He was gracious enough to save police the trouble of arresting him by killing himself at the scene. The shooter bought the gun legally from an Alabama pawnshop, despite his history of mental illness.

So, I was all caught up, until the next day. Some guy in my neighborhood in Los Angeles sat on a bench and started firing a gun into the air. The police showed up, and demanded that he drop the weapon. He didn't. He raised it toward them. And they shot him. Dead. This was across the street from a Starbucks I occasionally patronize, and a couple miles from my kids' school, just a little something to bring the insanity close to home.

Then I was caught up, until an August 2015 shooting in Roanoke, Virginia, where a mentally unstable former employee of a local TV station killed a reporter and her cameraman, on camera, with a Glock handgun he bought legally from a Virginia dealer.

Then I was caught up, until October, when a 20-year-old walked into a community college in Oregon and killed 10 people while wounding 7. Police found 6 weapons at the scene, and 7 more at his home. The guns were bought legally.

Ok, all caught up, until late November, when a trailer park loner killed 3, including a police officer, and wounded 7 at a Planned Parenthood facility in Colorado Springs.

Finally, all caught up, until early December. As I was re-writing this chapter with the TV on, suddenly there was breaking news about two individuals -- a husband and wife -- who went on a rampage at a San Bernardino facility that served people with developmental disabilities, killing 14 people and wounding 21. And while this turned out to be an act of terrorism, the shooters arrived with an arsenal that included rifles, handguns, three remote-controlled pipe bombs, and four high-capacity .223 caliber rifle magazines. And that's just what police found at the scene. A search of their SUV uncovered around 1400 .223 caliber rounds, 200 9-millimeter rounds, two .223 assault rifles, and two 9-millimeter pistols. After searching their home, police found another 2000 9 millimeter rounds, more than 2500 .223 rounds, several hundred long rifle rounds, 12 pipe bombs, and tools to construct IEDs. The husband was an American citizen. The guns and ammo were bought in the U.S., legally, some by a friend of one of the shooters.

Per a report by Lawrence O'Donnell on MSNBC, a study by a professor at the University of Alabama looked at data from 171 countries from 1966 to 2012. The study found that the United States had, by far, the most public mass shootings, with 90 during the 46-year period. That's 5 times as many as the next country on the list, the Philippines, with 18. Although the U.S. accounts for less than 5% of the world's population, we accounted for 31% of mass shootings.

Statistics vary but, depending on whom you believe, there have been between 62 and 181 school shootings since Columbine. And more than three-quarters of the guns were obtained legally. But the truly insane part of this is that we debate the stats and the causes instead of freaking out over the fact that PEOPLE ARE SHOOTING KIDS AT SCHOOL!

According to a 2014 article in *USA Today*, guns kill or hurt 20 kids a day. And yet our national outrage at murdered children didn't provide the president and Democrats with enough political cover to revisit the Assault Weapons Ban, a 10-year provision passed by Congress in 1994 and signed into law by President Clinton. It expired in 2004. There wasn't even a conversation about banning extended clip magazines. I guess the argument is that it would place an unnecessary burden on the homicidal maniac, forcing him to reload, and infringing on his freedom to shoot as many people as possible. Still, many, including a well-known actor, think the answer is that guns be allowed in schools. Excellent. Arm the security guards. Arm the teachers. Arm the janitors. Arm the lunch ladies. I guarantee the kids won't bitch about there being too many vegetables on their plates. Hell, let's just arm the kids, too. Turn the veggie battle into a fair fight -- High Noon in the cafeteria.

It's become sadly predictable that, whenever a shooting occurs, the NRA and their Republican enablers will immediately hide behind the skirts of the 2nd Amendment, defending our God-given right as Americans to buy all the guns we want. Yet, this was never its intent. Per Warren Burger, former Supreme Court Justice, and a conservative, appointed by Richard Nixon:

> *"The Gun Lobby's interpretation of the Second*
> *Amendment is one of the greatest pieces of fraud,*
> *I repeat the word fraud, on the American people by*
> *special interest groups that I have ever seen in my lifetime.*
> *The real purpose of the Second Amendment*
> *was to ensure that state armies – the militia –*

> would be maintained for the defense of the state. The very language of the Second Amendment refutes any argument that it was intended to guarantee every citizen an unfettered right to any kind of weapon he or she desires."

So, it's not a 2nd Amendment thing. The other NRA dodge is that it's not an automatic weapons problem, or an extended clip problem; it's a mental health problem. But here's the problem with that argument: it's horseshit. Crazy isn't an American thing. Crazy is a human thing. Armed and crazy is an American thing. The U.S. hasn't cornered the world market on people dealing with family crisis, heartbreak, loneliness, anonymity, sexual frustration, alienation, or rage. What we have cornered the market on is their ability to obtain maximum killing power when they pop off.

The other argument is that it's a privacy issue, the fear being that if the freedom-hating, monolithic U.S. government knew who had what weapons, they could just roll into town with a list of how many guns Buford's got hidden under the floorboards, and confiscate the hell out of his freedom. Interesting how the same people who criticize the federal government for being a bloated, incompetent bureaucracy simultaneously fear it for being organized enough to plot an attack against its own citizens. Despite the loopy statement from hog-castrating junior Senator Joanie Ernst, from the great state of Iowa, (well, ok, from Iowa) that her unregistered gun will protect her from the day the government decides to take away her freedom, it really won't.

Face it -- the government knows more about you than Santa Claus, and not just if you've been naughty or nice. They know your name, address, and Social Security number. They gave you your Social Security number. They collect your taxes. They know if you're single, married, or divorced, how much money you make, what your mortgage payment is and what kind of porn you like. They know if you've ever been arrested and, if so, they've got your mug shot and fingerprints. They issued your birth certificate, driver's license, and will issue your death certificate. They know what you look like, where you work, where you travel, what kind of car you drive, how many kids you have and where they go to school. They can track your phone calls, texts, emails, tweets, Snapchats, and Instagrams. They know if you're on Tinder or Grindr and, if you're Anthony Weiner, they know what your dick looks like. They know what you buy, where you shop, how much you spend, and who your friends are. They've got records on you from birth to death. And insurance company actuarial tables have the odds on when that will be. So there's an over/under on your life span. Between government records, market research, data mining, and all the personal information you gave out on Facebook, they can profile the hell out of you. Do you really think the only thing securing your freedom is whether they know if you own a Bushmaster?

No matter how far off the grid you think you are, unless you live in a tree house, don't work or pay taxes, farm or kill your own food, brew your own alcohol or grow your own dope, you're on their radar. And, frankly, who cares? If you're just a citizen minding your own business where do you get the arrogance to think the government gives a rat's ass about you? Do you really think you and your gun collection are the only things standing in the way of tyranny?

This isn't 1776, when a musket was the great equalizer. An armed citizenry couldn't hold off the fictional American military attack the paranoid Ernsts of the world live in such desperate fear of. And if the million-man Korean army suddenly landed on the west coast, or if space aliens traversed millions of light years to colonize this obscure little dump, despite the apocalyptic fantasies in movies like *Red Dawn* or *The 5th Wave,* I don't think they'd be defeated by a ragtag bunch of plucky, heavily-armed teenagers.

The framers of the Constitution created an amendable document based on the foresight that the world changes. And it has changed. It's now possible for every American to own his or her own weapon of mass destruction. And, yet, the great unlettered still justify arming themselves to the teeth by namedropping the founding fathers. But here's the thing about the founding fathers: they're everything these people despise.

They were educated men. They wrote books. Travelled to Europe. Liked wine. Weren't all down with Jesus. Or God. They were Francophiles. Schooled in Athenian democracy. Committed civil disobedience. Thirty-five had legal training. They were products of enlightenment thinking, read classical literature and history, challenged the church, and embraced Renaissance humanism. Two were scientists. Four were physicians. One was a college president. Of the Declaration signers, seven went to Harvard, and three went to William and Mary, Yale, and Penn. Two others attended Oxford and Cambridge. Granted, some owned slaves and didn't think women were ready to handle the vote, but it's not always easy to think yourself out of your cultural zeitgeist.

Despite the delusional terrorist rhetoric about destroying the Great Satan and establishing a caliphate in the U.S., my guess is they're not going to pull it off. Sharia Law is not coming to a town near you. There are no armies, foreign or domestic that are going to stage a U.S. takeover. Yet, every time there's a shooting, NRA Executive Vice President Wayne LaPierre steps in front of the cameras and bleats, "the only thing that stops a bad guy with a gun is a good guy with a gun" -- an argument that stinks worse than an old lady's perfume. When Ronald Reagan was shot he was surrounded by a phalanx of armed Secret Service agents who were specifically trained to prevent the one thing they failed to prevent.

It's also a smokescreen for the big lie justifying the NRA's existence. The NRA was founded in 1871 by Northern Civil War veterans who were disappointed by their troops' lack of marksmanship. Their primary goal was to "promote and encourage rifle shooting on a scientific basis." They don't represent 21st century minutemen. They're not a gun owners' lobby. They're a gun manufacturers' lobby.

In 2010 the NRA received $71 million in donations, much of it coming from manufacturers of assault weapons. 74% of their funding comes from corporations. According to Firearm Industry Statistics, there are 465 gun manufacturers in the U.S. The number of guns manufactured in the U.S. increased from 2.9 million in 2001 to almost 5.5 million in 2010. In 2013, guns and ammo sales rose to an estimated $14.7 billion. The NRA isn't fighting for the rights of the average American to own a 30-clip magazine. They're fighting for the rights of gun manufacturers to make and sell them, both in the U.S. and abroad. That's why they spend millions each year to make sure the politicians they bought remain in office.

Between homicides and suicides, there are over 30,000 firearm deaths in the U.S. each year. There are enough statistics to demonstrate that when you take anger, jealousy, road rage, heartbreak, unemployment, money problems, drugs, alcohol, economic inequality, racism, desperation, lonely, hormonal teenagers, a fame-obsessed culture, and the rage that manifests itself daily on the Internet, and then add lethal weapons, you get a recipe for murder. Premeditated or not. But what happens when you factor in human carelessness and good, old-fashioned American stupidity. These headlines were compiled over just the last few years, demonstrating that we're not just armed and dangerous; we're armed and dumb.

Brooklyn Dad Shoots Daughter While Cleaning Handgun

*Riverside Deputies Probe Teen's Shooting
Of 9-Year-Old Brother*

*Jose Canseco Accidentally Shoots
Off Finger While Cleaning His Gun*

*Toddler Accidentally Shoots Army Veteran Mom
Dead As She Changes Diaper*

*Utah Girl, 12, Accidentally Shot Dead By Sibling
After Church Talk On Love For Family*

*Illinois Teen Fatally Shoots Himself
While Chatting With Friend On FaceTime*

*Utah Hunter Killed After Friend Slips In Mud,
Fires Shotgun Into His Back*

*Idaho Mom Shot Dead By 2-Year-Old Son
Was Shopping With Christmas Present From Her Husband –
A Purse To Conceal Her Gun*

Police Officer Accidentally Shoots Himself In Elevator

*Florida Toddler Fatally Shoots Himself In The Chest
After Finding Father's Loaded Firearm In Car*

*Atlanta Girl, 6, Fatally Shoots Self
With Gun Found in Sofa*

*17-Year-Old Boy Shot, Killed, During
Russian Roulette Game*

*Michigan Republican Official Fatally Shoots Herself
In Eye While Adjusting Gun In Her Bra Holster*

Toddler Wounds Both Parents With One Shot From Handgun

3-Year-Old Shot In Face While Playing With A Gun

*St. Louis Woman Accidentally Kills Herself
With Gun She Bought For Possible Ferguson Unrest*

Oklahoma Honor Student Shot in Back
Playing Ding Dong Ditch

Florida Grandmother Shoots 7-Year-Old Grandson,
Mistaking Him For Burglar

Florida Woman Fatally Shoots Her Daughter
After Confusing Her For An Intruder

Florida 2-Year-Old Fatally Shoots Himself
After Finding Gun In Dad's Car

Father Accidentally Shoots Son In Face

Man Accidentally Shoots Woman During
"Freaky Sex"

19-Year-Old Father Of Two Accidentally
Kills Himself While Taking Selfie
With Gun to his Head

Washington State Police Officer
Shoots Sister With Dad's Gun

Man Accidentally Shoots
Son Outside Gun Store

Gun Goes Off In Altoona
Church During Easter Vigil

Boy Shoots Through Bedroom Window,
Kills Friend Trying to Wake Him

Yonkers Girl, 4, Dies Days
After Shooting Herself In Family's Home

Florida Man Threatens to Shoot Wife's Dog,
Accidentally Shoots Self In Face

Florida Man Shoots Self in Butt

Georgia Man Shoots Self in Penis

*Dallas Man Celebrating 21st Birthday
Accidentally Shoots Himself*

Texas 3-Year-Old Boy Accidentally Shoots Himself

*Idaho St. University Professor Shoots
Self in Foot During Class*

*Michigan Man Accidentally Shoots Self
in Hand While Killing Dog*

*Iowa Cop Accidentally Shoots Self
and Another Officer*

*Fresno Teen Shoots Himself Trying To Scare
Girlfriend And New Boyfriend*

*South Carolina Toddler Shoots Grandmother
With Gun He Finds in Back Seat of Car*

*Gun Seller Dad's 3-Year-Old Shot
By 4-Year-Old Neighbor*

*5 Hurt in Accidental Shooting
At Waldorf Astoria Wedding*

*Tulane University Student Accidentally
Shoots, Kills Boyfriend*

*Man at "Muslim Free" Gun Shop
Accidentally Shoots Himself*

2-Year-Old Boy Accidentally Shoots and Kills His Father

*Texas Man Shot When Bullet He Fired
Ricochets Off Armadillo And Strikes His Head*

*Man Caught Urinating on Brooklyn Street
Shoots Himself In Groin While Trying to Ditch Gun*

*L.A. Deputy Accidentally Shoots
Co-worker During Camping Trip*

Chicago Boy Fatally Shoots Brother

*2 Shot During "Old West" Gunfight Reenactment
in Tombstone*

*Gun Safety Instructor Accidentally Shoots
Pastor During Class*

*Woman Critically Injured When Drunk Man's Gun
Goes Off in Seattle Movie Theater*

*Man Accidentally Shoots Self in Foot
At Bass Pro Shop*

*Houston Boy, 4, To Be Buried in Ironman
Suit After Accidentally Shooting Himself
in Head With Grandfather's Gun*

*12-Year-Old Georgia Boy Accidentally
Shoots Self While Mom at Home*

*Pro-Gun Florida Mom Accidentally Shot
By 4-Year-Old Son*

*Dog Named Trigger Steps on Shotgun
Shoots Owner While Hunting*

Arkansas Dog Eats 17 Rounds of Live Ammo

Relax, the dog's ok. After what I imagine was some explosive diarrhea.

Forget about childproofing the house. We may need to adult-proof the country to stop us from committing slow national suicide. Or maybe just employ some common sense. You want to own guns? Fine. Given the seemingly constant state of fear we live in, it's not surprising that people feel better having a gun in the house to protect their family. It doesn't actually work out that way, as most statistics reveal that more family members are shot than intruders. But if it makes you feel safer, get a gun. Get two. Get ten. Get thirteen, like the Oregon shooter. Own 'em. Clean 'em. Shoot 'em. Show 'em off to your friends. Go plink beer bottles off the fence, blast targets at a gun range, shoot clay pigeons or ducks out of the sky, deer in the woods, rattlesnakes in the desert, or rats at the dump. Shoot anything you like. Just lock up the guns when you're done, and don't bring them to church, the mall, the park, or leave them in the car. And put the damn safety on. And keep them away from the kids, and your dog. Pretend it's your pot stash or your porn collection. And accept the need for common sense regulations.

We've already managed to place reasonable restrictions on our ability to procure weapons of mass destruction without neutering the country. You can't get a surface-to-air missile on Amazon. You can't stock the Costco cart with hand grenades. No husband wakes up on his birthday, is blindfolded by his wife and lead outside, where he's surprised by the sight of his brand new M1 tank tied up with a big red bow. Despite Jesus' plea to shoot the peacemakers, the kiddies don't get assault weapons for Christmas. (Although I saw some pretty realistic facsimiles in a gift shop at Universal CityWalk, in L.A. The perfect souvenir for your visit to Hollywood.)

There's enough evidence, both domestically and internationally, to prove that stronger gun laws decrease gun violence. Case in point: a 2013 study comparing death rates by state, which concluded that suicide and homicide rates were significantly lower in states with the most gun laws, including stronger background checks. Despite NRA misdirection and outright lies, it's not a slippery slope. The only slippery slope is with those who buy that argument, who slip from the fear of regulation down the rabbit hole of paranoia.

We need a responsible, intelligent national dialogue on this issue from every conceivable point of view. Of course, that will never happen. For decades, Republicans have blocked any attempt to appropriate money for the Center for Disease Control and Prevention to study the causes of gun violence. And they will always get out front after any shooting with the all-purpose disclaimer that more regulation won't solve the problem. And they're right. No single piece of legislation will ever solve this problem, because there is no single problem. We have too many guns, a culture of violence, a competitive way of life that can result in economic hardship and stress, different social conditions in the suburbs than in the cities. No mental health system in the world can screen out every potential shooter. And you can't arrest someone for seeming to be crazy enough to go on a rampage. It's simple to suggest we place armed guards at every school. But an assailant determined enough to carry out a mass shooting might also have enough guile to start killing at the other end of the school, where the guard isn't. And, of course, it's not just schools; it malls, movie theaters, restaurants, parks, and sidewalks.

There's no panacea. You just do everything you can, on every front, to limit the carnage. Universal background checks. Close the gun show loophole. Reinstate the Assault Weapons Ban. Make it at least as tough to buy a gun, as it is to get a driver's license. But none of these things are going to happen. At least as long as the NRA can point their most dangerous weapon at members of Congress: the threat of a primary challenge.

No Americans died from Ebola and yet the country went into a total meltdown in 2014. In the past we've freaked out over bird flu and swine flu. If some disease were killing tens of thousands of Americans every year, people would be storming Washington, demanding action. Hazmat suit sales would be through the roof. But as long as the epidemic is guns, and not germs, we still can't mobilize the political will to do anything about it. Maybe we need to rename it "gun flu" to get Congress to act. Well, at least their version of action. President Reagan and his press secretary James Brady were shot in 1981, and it took until 1993 to pass The Brady Bill, mandating federal background checks for gun purchases. And even then it had to be introduced twice in the House.

Even though, in early 2016, President Obama issued a series of executive actions widening the scope of background checks to include gun show and Internet sellers, along with hiring additional FBI agents, and providing additional funds for mental health services, it's not going to make a real dent in the problem. So, for the moment, I guess we'll have to console ourselves with the laws we have.

So, if some disturbed loner wakes up tomorrow morning and thinks: "Life's just not worth living. I've got no friends. No job. Girls don't like me. I've got a face like a pizza that's been left out in the sun. I don't have the brains or talent to do anything interesting in life. I'm bored with jerking off to Internet porn. So, maybe I'll just kill myself. But that's too anonymous. I think I'll take a few dozen random folks with me. So, I'm going to get in the car, drive down to the gun shop, and buy me a Bushmaster and a ton of ammo so the world can pay for my misery, and remember my name," he can't. He has to wait for a background check, which could take up to several minutes. Because that's the way we roll in America.

CHAPTER FIVE

DUMBF⬛CK CULTURE

BREAD AND CIRCUSES

*"No one ever went broke underestimating
the good taste of the American public."*
H.L. Mencken

In the 1st Century A.D. Roman satirist and poet, Juvenal, used the term "bread and circuses" to describe the tactics Roman politicians used to win votes and stay in power by handing out free wheat and providing circus entertainment. Perhaps it's true that the more things change the more they remain the same. Some 2000 years later, the modern-day equivalent of bread and circuses is Burger King's 1230 calorie *Triple Whopper with Cheese*, and the latest superhero movie.

American culture, a term that, at times, seems oxymoronic is, at best schizophrenic. On the one hand, we're the soul of creativity. American music. American movies. American cars. American technology. We may outsource our manufacturing, but Google, Apple, Microsoft, Facebook -- American companies.

Although every country has its indigenous folk music, American music is all over the world. Gospel, folk, country, rock 'n' roll, blues, R&B, jazz, rock, funk, soul, disco (belated apologies for that), punk (maybe that was the UK; it's debatable), metal, grunge, rap, hip-hop. I'm not sure I get the hipster neofolk movement, or the Amish beards, but that may just be a matter of age. Every generation has that unique thing they all conform to, to show how nonconformist they are. You know, before they get sucked down in the undertow of work, marriage, family, mortgages, old age, and death. Although the beards really look dumb.

We're inventors and innovators; yet, simultaneously, we're the soulless creators of mindless crap. We take excellence and mediocritize it. We turn jazz into smooth jazz, rock into soft rock. Give us something unique and we'll wring every nuance out of it then reconstitute it in some trivialized, homogenized form for mass consumption.

We take the buttery, flaky perfection that is the croissant, put it through the American trivializer and, voila! The 32 grams of fat, 1060 mg of sodium, 180 grams of cholesterol Burger King *Croissan'wich*. Granted the original French version isn't exactly health food. But if something's going to kill you, would you rather be kissed to death or have your heart blown up by a culinary IED?

We take something as sublime as real Italian pizza, crucify it, then resurrect it as a goopy mass of processed cheese, dolloped over a crime scene of bloody tomato sauce splayed out on a slab of greasy bread. Then we give it a snappy name like *Pizzone, Pizza Rolls,* or *Triple Cheese Covered Stuffed Crust*. That last gastronomic conflagration is from Pizza Hut, and features not just regular cheese on top, but Parmesan, cheddar and aged Asiago baked into the crust. Because if anything is emblematic of the good life, it's mass quantities of cheese, inside bread, then topped with more cheese.

But it's not just our food. As I sit here writing in a Glendale mall Barnes and Noble, there's music being piped in. Bach? Hendrix? Sinatra? Willie Nelson? Miles Davis? B.B. King? Nope. It's an excruciatingly painful, horribly arranged series of instrumental '60s TV theme songs. As a child of the '60s, those songs are hard-wired into my brain, but were buried so deep I thought they'd never rise back up, like nuclear waste in the desert. Yet, here they are, playing on a loop, over and over, and it never fucking stops.

Crap food. Toxic music. Even pop psychology and religion. We take the human impulse toward self-knowledge, and reconstitute it as EST, The Forum, and Scientology. We pervert the 5000-year-old spiritual discipline of Yoga into a weight loss regimen and an excuse to buy cute, clingy stretch pants. And then there's our affectation for New Age religion, which is to actual religion as light jazz is to Coltrane: Astrology, palm reading, Phrenology, past life regression, astral projection, tarot, numerology, crystals, psychics, and mediums who talk to the dead. Though, unless you're talking about The Grateful Dead, whoever said the actual dead were hanging around waiting for a call? We get all gooey at the thought of being able to chat with grandpa and think all we need is a dark room, incense, weird music, and people holding hands around a table, all presided over by a fat chick in a peasant dress and headscarf.

I guess that's why Americans spend about $1 billion a year on psychics. Not to mention the multi-millions shelled out on motivational life coaches, transformation specialists, personal empowerment gurus, human potential advocates, self-actualization counselors, or spiritual messengers to help them Discover their Inner Warrior, Revitalize their Life, Unleash their Power, and Be Their Own Miracle during an intense Interpersonal Mental Colonic Psychic Healing Encounter Weekend.

Then there's *The Secret*, 198 pages of "if you believe it, you can achieve it" platitudes conflating financial success with spirituality. To date, it's sold over 19 million copies worldwide, been translated into 46 languages, and spawned *The Secret Daily Teachings*, *The Secret (Extended Edition) DVD*, *The Secret Gratitude Book*, and *The Secret Soundtrack*. For a secret, it's certainly gotten a lot of publicity.

Even publishing, an industry that's traditionally been a vehicle for the best and brightest fiction and non-fiction writers is now just another marketing tool. The Kardashians have published eight books, including a cookbook and two novels. Paris Hilton is a published author. Bill O'Reilly has written *Killing Kennedy*, *Killing Lincoln*, *Killing Patton*, *Killing Jesus*, and *Killing Reagan*. How about *Killing Journalism?*

The American penchant for producing garbage for profit spans all areas of our culture. Mass entertainment has gone from a product that reached the masses to one that reflects the taste of the masses. The media conglomerates are essentially vertically integrated perpetual motion profit machines. Not that the original studio moguls were Renaissance patrons of the arts. Louis B. Mayer famously quipped: "If you've got a message, call Western Union."

However, they knew that box office success and exploring the human condition weren't mutually exclusive. The movies they made reflected the complexities of life. Now they reflect Comic-Con and the testosterone-laced superhero fantasies of adolescent boys, or the Disneyfied romantic yearnings of teenage girls. One could make the case that our 60% national divorce rate is partially due to the latter notion being dangled before the starry eyes of impressionable young women. They dream of marrying Prince Charming only to discover that if he comes galloping in on a white horse it's usually just to get laid. In time, he'll trade in the horse for a sandwich, a beer, and a La-Z-Boy.

Don't get me wrong; growing up I had a stack of comics under my bed. Superman. Batman. Archie. I loved reading them. When I was 8. Soon after, when I learned more words, I graduated to *Mad Magazine, National Lampoon*, and eventually actual books, for the simple reason that I wanted to learn shit.

I also loved movies. Weekends were spent in dark theaters watching monster movies featuring that classic Ray Harryhausen animation. It was a great way to spend a rainy Sunday. When I was 8. When I got older I discovered films. (A pretentious distinction, I know, but I'm not sure how else to distinguish between entertainment that titillates and art that communicates.)

Discovering films was like discovering literature. They were often grounded in the American archetype of the quiet, self-effacing hero who wrestled with a moral dilemma, but did the right thing in the end, like Gary Cooper in *High Noon*. But they also explored our dark side, with the protagonist who'd lost his sense of purpose, but ultimately re-discovered it, like Bogart in *Casablanca*. In either case, the hero's struggle was a journey of self-discovery, one that reflected our own. American films weren't afraid to challenge our assumptions about ourselves, or shine a light on our weaknesses, prejudices, or hypocrisy. Think of *Gentlemen's Agreement, The Apartment, Guess Who's Coming to Dinner, Black Like Me, In the Heat of the Night*.

That all began to change in 1975 with the release of *Jaws*. This was a eureka moment for the studios, and ushered in a change in their mindset from movies as art form to movies as profit machine. But the real paradigm shift came in 1978 with the first *Superman* film, which grossed $300 million worldwide. The first seven *Superman* movies grossed over $1.5 billion. The genre hit the stratosphere with Tim Burton's dark take on *Batman*, also in 1978, which grossed over $400 million. Since 1978, the 100 highest-grossing superhero movies have made over $13.5 billion.

Suddenly, the movie hero changed from the tough iconoclast to the hapless victim and social outcast who, through some scientific fluke or planetary explosion, is infused with extraordinary abilities and suddenly gets the urge to leap around in Spandex. He went from someone who was a reflection of us to someone who's stronger, smarter and more powerful than us, and who, like some super-powered Jesus, will come along to save us.

But, studios aren't only in the superhero business. They also fill the culture with action movies. The 7 *Fast and Furious* movies have grossed almost $4 billion worldwide, with the latest sequel reaching the $1 billion mark in just 17 days. (*Fast and Furious Supercharged* is now a ride at Universal Studios. I don't think there are plans for a *Citizen Kane Supercharged*, unless it's a metaphor for the American dream.)

The other revelatory moment for studios came in 1992, with the release of *Aladdin*. It grossed over $500 million, worldwide. But the real discovery was that if you made an animated film voiced by famous actors, and sprinkled with enough jokes that flew over the heads of kids but landed with parents, you could sell four tickets instead of two; double the fun, double the profits. And that's not including the merchandising, and DVD sales.

And then there are the Rom-Coms and goofball comedies, our modern versions of the screwball comedies of the '30s and '40s. Movies like *It Happened One Night, My Man Godfrey, The Front Page, His Girl Friday,* among many others. They were intelligent, cleverly plotted, and featured smart, rapid-fire dialogue. Occasionally they even had an element of social critique.

And what do we have? In March 2015, promos starting appearing for the movie: *Paul Blart Mall Cop 2*. It was produced by Sony, which spent $30 million on the film. Why, you might ask, was it necessary to make *PBMC2*? Had they not plumbed the depths of the Blart character, portrayed by comic Kevin James, in the original *PBMC*? Why would one become a mall cop? Did he have career goals and unrealized dreams? Would he get the girl in the end? Was America really pining for the next fat-guy-fall-down *PBMC*, the way *Godfather* fans ached for *Godfather II* (and pained over *Godfather III)?* No. It was because *PBMC* cost $26 million to produce and grossed $183 million, worldwide. Hence *PBMC2*.

Not that character-based, albeit star-driven films, aren't released by the studios. They are. But it's a matter of balance. And that balance affects the culture. As former co-founder of CAA and one-time head of Universal, Ron Meyer said: "A critical hit is great when it happens… It's great to win awards and make films that you're proud of… but your first obligation is to make money, and then worry about being proud of what you do." Or as Barry Diller, former head of Paramount put it: "Movies stink because of greater corporate interests." Yet, most people in the business will just shrug and quip, "Hey, "it's not show art. It's show business."

Superheroes, cartoons, and the inevitable sequels. Because if it's good enough to make, it's good enough to remake. Just look at how studio releases have changed over the years. These are just some examples. There are dozens more that illustrate the point.

MOVIES OF THE '30S

Gone With the Wind, All Quiet on the Western Front, Modern Times, Treasure Island, Stagecoach, It Happened One Night, Mr. Smith Goes to Washington, Scarface, The 39 Steps, Lost Horizon, Grand Hotel, Mutiny on the Bounty, Mr. Deeds Goes to Town, Gunga Din, City Lights, Little Caesar.

MOVIES OF THE '40S

Citizen Kane, Casablanca, It's a Wonderful Life, The Maltese Falcon, The Treasure of the Sierra Madre, The Best Years of Our Lives, All The King's Men, Gentlemen's Agreement, The Lost Weekend, A Tree Grows in Brooklyn, Sullivan's Travels, The Grapes of Wrath, The Third Man.

MOVIES OF THE '50S

On The Waterfront, Sunset Boulevard, Rear Window, Touch of Evil, Rebel Without a Cause, The African Queen, 12 Angry Men, High Noon, A Streetcar Named Desire, From Here To Eternity, East of Eden, Blackboard Jungle, Giant, Marty, The Bridge On The River Kwai, Strangers on a Train, Sweet Smell of Success, Witness For the Prosecution, A Face in the Crowd.

MOVIES OF THE '60S

Dr. Strangelove, To Kill a Mockingbird, Midnight Cowboy, Bonnie and Clyde, The Apartment, Breakfast at Tiffany's, The Graduate, 2001: A Space Odyssey, In the Heat of the Night, Cool Hand Luke, The Manchurian Candidate, Easy Rider, Inherit the Wind, The Hustler.

MOVIES OF THE '70S

The Godfather, The Godfather Part II, One Flew Over the Cuckoo's Nest, Apocalypse Now, Chinatown, A Clockwork Orange, Mean Streets, All the President's Men, The Deer Hunter, Taxi Driver, Kramer vs. Kramer, Shampoo, MASH, Catch 22, Five Easy Pieces, The Conversation, Coming Home, Straw Dogs, Carnal Knowledge, Network.

MOVIES OF THE '80S

Raging Bull, Platoon, Do The Right Thing, Full Metal Jacket, The Big Chill, Scarface, Crimes and Misdemeanors, Field of Dreams, The Breakfast Club, The Color of Money, Blade Runner, Dead Poets Society, The Color Purple.

A PARTIAL LIST OF STUDIO RELEASES
1990-2015

Darkman, Captain America, Teenage Mutant Ninja Turtles II, The Rocketeer, Batman, Teenage Mutant Ninja Turtles III, The Meteor Man, The Fantastic Four, The Crow, Batman Forever, Mighty Morphin Power Rangers, Darkman II, The Crow: City of Angels, Darkman III, Batman and Robin, The Crow: Salvation, X-Men, Spiderman, X2: X-Men United, Hulk, The League of Extraordinary Gentlemen, The Amazing Spider-Man 2, Catwoman, Batman Returns, Batman Forever, Batman and Robin, Batman Begins, The Dark Knight, The Dark Knight Rises, Batman: Mask of the Phantasm, Batman v. Superman: Dawn of Justice, Superman, Superman II, Superman III, Superman Returns, Man of Steel, Supergirl, Fantastic Four, Ghost Rider, Fantastic Four: Rise of the Silver Surfer, Iron Man, The Incredible Hulk, Watchmen, X-Men Origins: Wolverine, Iron Man 2, Jonah Hex, The Green Hornet, Thor, X-Men: First Class, Green Lantern, Captain America: The First Avenger, The Avengers, The Amazing Spiderman, Iron Man 3, Man of Steel, The Wolverine, Thor: The Dark World, Captain America: The Winter Soldier, X-Men: Days of Future Past, Guardians of the Galaxy, Avengers: Age of Ultron, Fantastic Four Reboot, Captain America 3, Ant-Man, Fantastic Four, Captain America: Civil War, The Fantastic Four 2, Thor: Ragnarok, Avengers: Infinity War Part I, Captain Marvel, Avengers: Infinity War Part II, The Amazing Spider-Man 3, The Amazing Spider-Man 4.

A PARTIAL LIST OF SEQUELS 2014-2020

Hotel Transylvania 2, The SpongeBob Movie: Sponge Out of Water, Pitch Perfect 2, Crouching Tiger Hidden Dragon: The Green Legend, The Second Best Exotic Marigold Hotel, Who Framed Roger Rabbit 2, Hot Tub Time Machine 2, Magic Mike XXL, Kung Fu Panda 3, Minions, The Hunger Games: Mockingjay – Part 2, Taken 3, Mad Max: Fury Road, Jurassic World, Mission: Impossible – Rogue Nation, Terminator Genisys, Paranormal Activity: The Ghost Dimension, Star Wars: Episode VII – The Force Awakens, Prometheus 2, Independence Day 2, Teenage Mutant Ninja Turtles 2, Avatar 2, Prisoners of the Sun, Ride Along 2, Finding Dory, The Nut Job 2, Untitled Smurfs Movie, Star Trek 3, War of the Planet of the Apes, The Chronicles of Narnia: The Silver Chair, Alvin and the Chipmunks: The Road Chip, Beverly Hills Cop 4, Transformers 5, Ice Age 5, Resident Evil: The Final Chapter, X-Men Apocalypse, Guardians of the Galaxy 2, Avatar 3, Fantastic Four 2, The Lego Batman Movie, The Croods 2, Pacific Rim 2, Untitled Wolverine Sequel, How to Train Your Dragon 3, Despicable Me 3, Toy Story 4, Pirates of the Caribbean: Dead Men Tell No Tales, Goonies, Gremlins 3, Ghostbusters, Top Gun 2, My Big Fat Greek Wedding 2. Zoolander 2.

So much for exploring the human condition. It's about franchises, brand recognition, product placement, corporate tie-ins, and merchandising. Not that there haven't been great studio films produced in all those years. But the superhero movies are a part of the equation in a way they never were before. And it's not that these movies aren't entertaining or well made. They are. Well, mostly... Still, it always amazes me when I overhear a group of adults talking about how the latest *Iron Man* was "fucking awesome."

Of course, the counter argument is that these movies bring out our inner child. But there's a difference between childlike innocence and childish immaturity. The former keeps a spirit of wonder alive in adults as we go through life and have experiences that beat the joy right out of us. The latter leads to adults who stand around talking about how the latest *Iron Man* was "fucking awesome."

Working in Hollywood, I understand that people can reach near sexual climax over big opening weekend numbers. But at least there's a reason for the excitement: money, and keeping their jobs, or delighting in the fact that some asshole will probably lose theirs. It's been said in Hollywood that friends don't want friends to fail. Friends want friends to die.

Another argument is that it's just harmless fantasy. What's wrong with that? Well, in one sense -- nothing. Given the popularity of Comic-Con, they've obviously touched a nerve. And there are talented, thoughtful people behind these movies. But a relentless wave of them has the long-term effect of dumbing down the culture.

They also send a message to look elsewhere for heroes, instead of looking within. George Lucas has talked about Luke Skywalker's journey in *Star Wars* being inspired by the work of Joseph Campbell, particularly *The Hero With a Thousand Faces*. Campbell understood that the hero's journey was a paradigm for our own. The demons he fought and the challenges he faced were inside him. But this idea doesn't exist in contemporary American culture.

We take our heroes straight up, as all-American icons. We see myth as history, not metaphor. Who else sends teams of Christian archaeologists scouring the Middle East looking for Noah's Ark? What's next? Christian astronauts blasting into space, searching for Kronos? If so, I fear for the universe, because instead of being guided by the *Star Trek* Prime Directive, they'll be armed with copies of the Bible translated into Klingon.

And then there's TV. At this point, I should confess that I've made a nice living for about 25 years working as a writer in sitcoms, which I know can be accused of being dumb. And there's a reason for that. Many of them are. I've produced over 300 episodes of half-hour TV. Written about 40 of them. Even directed one. I've worked on shows I've loved, shows I've liked, and shows I've worked on. I've gotten a few shows of my own on the air that have crashed and burned, and in the process have written dozens of pilots and had hundreds of meetings and pitches. And I can personally attest to the fact that it's not always easy to get the networks to raise the taste level or the intelligence bar.

The most popular network shows these days seem to be singing contests, dancing contests, dating contests, cooking contests, diet contests, ninja contests, even business contests. For the handful of real artists who have come off *American Idol* and *The Voice*, there have been hundreds of mimics, imitators, and wannabes who prove that you can possess a decent singing voice while having absolutely no originality, soul, or style whatsoever. Yet, each tryout brings hordes of wannabes, armed with a raging desire for their ticket to Hollywood. Fame, once tangentially related to talent and hard work, can now be fast-tracked by winning a reality show, or via a clever YouTube video or accidentally released sex tape.

The terms "reality star" and "YouTube star" have entered the nomenclature. Fame is something people seek for its own sake. Follow me! Friend me! Re-tweet me! We have Auto-Tune for singers with no voice. Now there's Auto-Fame for people with no talent. Even young hipster culture, which seems to be above it all, simultaneously chases fame via Instagram, Twitter, and YouTube. There are about 325 million Americans. We can't all be famous. Who'd be left to adore us? Though, I suppose we could outsource it.

And if the bar wasn't low enough, with reality TV there's no more bar. *Jersey Shore* ran for six seasons on MTV. Provocative in its time, it now seems quaint. A 2013 MTV show called *Buckwild*, about partying kids in West Virginia, only got cancelled when one of them died. And of course it's easy to take a blanket swipe at The Kardashians, but at this point it's like shooting Botoxed, big ass fish in a barrel. And although their show helped usher in the wave of voyeuristic TV in 2007, and just got renewed in a three-year, $80-million deal, it now seems like Shakespeare. Just a casual trip through the freak show in the Middle Earth regions of cable reveals shows like *River Monsters, Junkyard Empire, Alaskan Bush People, The Long Island Medium,* and my new favorite: *My 600-Pound Life.*

What other country would have a show about people who weigh over 600 pounds? What other country has people who weigh over 600 pounds! That's not just "I fell off my diet" fat. That's "I deep fried my neighbor and ate him" fat. How do we do this? Have we no shame left? There are kids starving all over the world and we've got people who stuff so much food down their gullets they have to be airlifted out of their bedrooms on a crane.

And then there was *19 Kids and Counting,* featuring the hyper-Christian Duggar family, who built a TV empire on the rock of their faith and their mom's log flume of a birth canal. Although the brand was tainted in May 2015, when a story broke that one of the Duggar boys was allegedly molesting girls from the time he was a teenager in Arkansas, some of the victims his own sisters. (I didn't realize child molestation was illegal in Arkansas. I thought it was mandatory.)

In any case, given the allegations, Duggar resigned his position as Vice President of The Family Research Council. Maybe he should have claimed that incest fell under the heading of family research. Or maybe it wouldn't have mattered. The show was soon cancelled, after which he was busted in the Ashley Madison hack.

But the real crime here, other than child molestation and an alleged 9-year cover up, is that these shows are on The Learning Channel. The Learning Channel? Exactly what are people learning other than to be morbidly obese, hyper-breeding, alleged child molesters? At least they should call it The Learnin' Channel, or maybe just Junkyard Empire.

Along with our actual crap diet is our steady diet of celebrity scandal, where the public failings of the rich and famous momentarily deflect our attention from the emptiness in our own lives. From the comings and goings of some politician's dick to the latest celebrity murder trial, we flit like hummingbirds from one diversion to the next, sucking the flower dry before zipping off to drink from another.

Basically, the media knows four stories: they're great; they're done; they're back; they're dead. We worship heroes, then in a twisted mash-up of envy and *schadenfreude*, revel in their fall from grace, only to stand up again and cheer at their redemption. Then, eventually, we spend a day or two chewing on the details of their death, unless it's Michael Jackson, in which case we collapse into a national state of mourning, along with 24/7 Action News Team coverage. As if one Jesus wasn't enough so we need to manufacture new ones. Maybe those in the media know that this meme is hard-wired into our collective unconscious, dating back to the heroes of Greek mythology.

Then there's the news. Once upon a time it arrived via the morning papers and the evening broadcast with the trusted male anchor. Traditions that now barely cling to life. Between websites, news aggregators, the blogosphere, social networks, and the Twitterverse, people stay informed by osmosis 24 hours a day. The upside is that we're always plugged in. The downside is that news, celebrity gossip, diet tips, ads, and movie promos are all served up on the screen like some mass information buffet. In 2013, there was a front-page article on the *L.A. Times* website about two researchers who received the Nobel Prize in Physics for discovering the God Particle. The article next to it: "Could Satan worship lower a mega mansion's value?" Science and superstition, side by side.

A quick glance at the front page of *The Huffington Post* revealed a shot of dead bodies lying in the street, and the headline "Heat Wave Kills Over 500 People in India." I take a moment for the "it's horrible but what can you do," nod to compassion, then look to the right at a picture of a suburban lawn, and an article on the "Do's and Don'ts of Backyard Landscaping." All info, no context, and seemingly no awareness of the juxtaposition of two, very distinct realities.

Then I check out the New York *Daily News* website. Where the headline might be is an ad in Spanish for Carefree Panty Liners. Below that is an ad for Western Union, then a headline about the funeral of a murdered Houston police officer. Right underneath, a story about the heir to the Frito Lay foundation being found dead in L.A., right next to an article, with 3 pictures, about Khloe Kardashian lasering off her "daddy" tramp stamp tattoo, right over an ad for Ford.

Another day on *Yahoo News*, the headline quotes Trump's latest word vomit, followed by an article about an Iran Revolutionary Guard commander who was killed in Syria. Below that, the headline: "Here's Why The PLO Just Condemned Howard Stern." The stories just meander from topic to topic, like a drunk staggering down the street. I didn't stop to read the piece, but the PLO/Stern story was baffling. First, who knew the PLO was still around? They seem like such quaint terrorists. So 20th century. And how did Howard get on their bad side? Did they form a dance troop and audition on *America's Got Talent*, only to get low marks?

Then I click on *The Daily Beast* and am immediately drawn to the headline: "Cher Is Not Impressed With Obama's ISIS War." Now, just as I did, take a moment to ponder that. Let it swirl around your brain like the aroma of a rich Burgundy. The first thing that hit me was that this was probably the first time in history the words Isis, Obama, and Cher were used in the same sentence. The piece went on to detail several recent tweets from the entertainer (born Cherilyn Sarkisian, as the writer felt important to note) suggesting that the president needed to take stronger military action to fight these terrorists. And while I doubt Cher is in on national security briefings, so I can't say how informed she is, by the tone of her tweets, she seems passionate. The article mentioned previous comments she'd made on the subject, then went on to state, "Cher's position on ISIS isn't as hawkish as, say, rapper Flavor Flav's, who has called for a large international coalition, led by the United States, to invade Syria and Iraq and crush the terror group." Apparently, someone who edits this site thought I not only needed to know what Cher thinks about ISIS, but for the piece to stack up as serious journalism, I'd need some perspective, so they included the rapper's take on the situation.

And then there are the excruciating puns -- puns being the idiot's poetry. One would think that respectable news organizations would avoid them, at least when reporting human tragedy. Maybe they're inspired by the famous *New York Post* headline: "Headless Body in Topless Bar." But at least that had wit. Just a quick glance at CNN online reveals a story about 431 people who died when a cruise ship capsized in China. The headline: "Deep Pain." Because the ocean's deep, and dying is painful. Then I check the *Daily News* site and notice a story about a husband who poisoned his wife with arsenic-laced milkshakes. The headline: "Shaky Marriage." As they said about computers at their inception: GIGO -- garbage in, garbage out.

It's possible that print won't even survive the first half of the 21st century. And while the traditional news icons have retained online respectability, others seem to dangerously straddle the newspaper/tabloid fault line. When I lived in New York, the *Daily News* was part of my routine. Writers like Jimmy Breslin,

Pete Hamill, and Mike Lupica captured the mood and pulse of the city. And those voices are still there. I still love the *Daily News*. But a cursory glance at their website reveals they've gone slightly postal, as in *New York Post-al.*

Scan the front page and the provocative headline language jumps out: "*Nightmare,*" "*bomb threat,*" "*sex,*" "*shoots,*" "*chokes,*" "*slams,*" "*freaks,*" "*rips,*" "*brutalized,*" "*fight,*" "*drug dealer,*" "*assault,*" "*crime,*" "*terror,*" "*slay.*" And everything is "*shocking.*" Not that there's ever been a day without crime and mayhem in New York, or anywhere else. The *Los Angeles Times* website has a section called *The Homicide Report*. But at some point we're not being informed so much as titillated, provoked, or scared out of our wits, and what suffers is any sense of context, or perspective.

Case in point: a *Daily News* headline reading: "NFL to Review Video That May Show Saints Linebacker Hitting Woman With Belt During 2013 Beach Brawl." Then, underneath the video, the caveat: "Warning. Graphic language." So, it's ok to watch a clip of someone whipping a woman with a belt, but before you do, you need a heads-up that the guy has a potty mouth.

Even TV news shows take reality and break it down to a black/white, left/right slugfest. Take any story from the past year: the protests in Ferguson over a cop killing a black guy; the protests in Staten Island over cops killing a black guy; the protests in Baltimore over a cop killing a black guy; the protests in Charleston over a deranged young racist killing black people in church. We get facts, and footage, along with the gang of usual suspects ringing in on either side. "It's the victim's fault for provoking the cops!" "It's the cops' fault for being overly aggressive and/or racist!" "It's the protestors' fault for making a bad situation worse or taking advantage of community outrage and playing to the media!" "It's the media's fault for being played!" And, in the case of Charleston, my favorite from the NRA, "it's the victims' fault for not having guns." In church.

Rarely do we get a sober dialogue on the many factors at the root of the problem: Racism, social inequality, an epidemic of street crime, good cops doing a tough job and losing their shit, bad cops on the rampage, the need for police/community communication, too many guns.

Ultimately, we get what we ask for. The culture has been dumbed down for our consumption because we consume it. Junk food wouldn't sell if we didn't eat it. Crap movies wouldn't get produced if we didn't pay to see them. Crap TV wouldn't get made if we didn't watch it. We're not only what we eat. We're also what we see and what we buy. Our culture is a reflection of who we are and how we think. We have met the enemy and he is us.

Whether it's food, news, music, movies, or TV, the public is being systematically fattened up and dumbed down by corporations that play to our basest instincts and desires. And while stupidity doesn't entirely break down along geographical lines; let's face it, some parts of the country are just dumberer than others.

CHAPTER SIX

DUMBF**CK STATES OF MIND

A FLYOVER ANALYSIS

Red States, Dumb States,
Fat States, Gun States,
Poor States, Sick States,
God States, Bummed States

Let's first dispense with the tired, prejudicial stereotype that all Southerners are dumb rednecks with fewer brain cells than teeth. It's not true. The three most inspiring Philosophy professors I had in college were Southern women. My Religion professor in grad school, one of the wisest people I've ever met, was a Texas Baptist. So, I know it's a cheap shot. A derogatory cliché proffered by urban elitists making value judgments about a group of people solely based on where they live and how they speak. Many of the greatest minds and creative talents in the country have come from the South.

Edgar Allen Poe, Margaret Mitchell, Mark Twain, Frederick Douglass, James Fenimore Cooper, William Faulkner, O Henry, Tennessee Williams, Robert Penn Warren, Erskine Caldwell, Richard Wright, Truman Capote, Lillian Hellman, James Agee, Harper Lee, Carson McCullers, Larry McMurtry, Eudora Welty, Pearl S. Buck, James Dickey, William Styron, Alice Walker, Maya Angelou, Cormac McCarthy, Ralph Ellison, Ann Rice, John Kennedy Toole, Horton Foote, Pat Conroy, Willa Cather, Hunter Thompson, Tom Wolfe, W.C. Handy, Scott Joplin, Jelly Roll Morton, Big Mama Thornton, Sister Rosetta Tharpe, Robert Johnson, Elmore James, Sonny Boy Williamson, Lightnin' Hopkins, Son House, J.B. Lenoir, Leadbelly, Bukka White, Robert Lockwood Jr., T-Bone Walker, Sam Phillips, Elvis Presley, Carl Perkins, Ike Turner, Jerry Lee Lewis, Chet Atkins, Mahalia Jackson, Billie Holiday, Ella Fitzgerald, Louis Armstrong, Nat King Cole, Lionel Hampton, Dizzy Gillespie, Bo Diddley, Fats Domino, Little Richard, John Lee Hooker, Jimmy Reed, Jimmy Rogers, Buddy Guy, Hubert Sumlin, Muddy Waters, Willie Dixon, Howlin' Wolf, B.B. King, Albert King, Freddie King, Otis Redding, James Brown, Aretha Franklin, Sam Cooke, Wilson Pickett, Al Green, Dr. John, Ray Charles, Alan Toussaint, Lowell George, Tom Petty, Duane Allman, Gregg Allman, Derek Trucks, Doyle Bramhall, Doyle Bramhall II, Jimmie Vaughan, Stevie Ray Vaughan, Johnny Winter, Edgar Winter, Janis Joplin, Willie Nelson, Waylon Jennings, Merle Haggard, Kris Kristofferson, Johnny Cash, Hank Williams, Thelonious Monk, John Coltrane, Mose Allison, Ornette Coleman, Ellis Marsalis, Wynton Marsalis, Branford Marsalis, Alvin Ailey, Robert Rauschenberg, Muhammad Ali, Rev. Dr. Martin Luther King, Julian Bond, Bill Moyers, Dan Rather, Don Henley, Bill Hicks, Steven Colbert, Zach Galifianakis, Gary Clark, Jr., and Jack Daniels. Just to randomly namedrop a few.

The South is the cradle of American music. Gospel, country, bluegrass, jazz, rock 'n' roll, rockabilly, Cajun, Zydeco, and, of course, the blues. Sure, it took the pain of slavery to give birth to it but, like a lotus rising from the mud, beauty can arise from ugliness. The South has given us 14 presidents, as well as artists, philosophers, teachers, poets, actors, athletes, doctors, scientists, entrepreneurs, journalists, and others in all walks of life who have not only excelled in their respective professions, but have expressed themselves eloquently about the human condition, while reflecting the subtleties of the Southern experience.

There's also something to be said for Southern grace and gentility. Even the term "bless his heart," referring to someone less fortunate yet who's trying their best, carries a uniquely Southern mix of compassion and pity. Even if the undercurrent is "don't you just feel awful for that poor bastard," it's said so sweetly.

And as far as its ugly past, while the South seems to have trademarked racism, it's ultimately the result of fear, stupidity, and the dark side of the human heart. And that transcends geography. So, it's grossly unfair and unjust to suggest that all Southerners are dumb. They're not.

It's the South that's dumb. As are many people in it.

OK, I'll hold for the outrage: how dare you categorize a single part of the country as a literal confederacy of dunces! You're right. Some of the brightest people I know are from the South. However, most of the brightest people I know aren't. And, yes, I know many of those I namedropped weren't technically from the South. But I'm not just talking about the geographical South. I'm talking about the red state, intellectual South. American stupidity isn't confined to one geographical area. The South is just its national headquarters -- the fertile crescent of the feeble-minded.

There are genuine (*gin-u-waaane*) shitkickers all over America. Alaska; well, you betcha. Utah. That's your Mormon central command. The word "moron" is built right in. Upset? Tough shit. An entire city and culture centered around a story about a magic angel who transmigrated to upstate New York, 1800 years after the death of Christ, just to reveal the location of some golden plates that would serve to translate a second gospel, like some Mormon Rosetta Stone? Please. And to whom was this revelation made? Joseph Smith. The L. Ron Hubbard of his day. Yeah, that happened, in reality. Because it's not possible that Smith was either delusional, or a con artist who made it all up. Besides, if you avoid alcohol, caffeine, and pre-marital sex just because a magic angel said so, you need to do a serious rethink.

And Texas. Well, as they say: "everything's bigger in Texas." Including the depth and breath of their stupidity. If, during a drought, your governor appeals to the citizenry to pray for rain, and a mob doesn't show up to physically remove him from office for being too goddamn dumb to govern, you leave yourself open to ridicule. As you do if you try to put creationism on equal footing with evolution in your school textbooks.

"I don't have no fancy, Ivy League education" should be an admission that one didn't have the brains to get into a top university and therefore shouldn't be trusted to operate heavy machinery, let alone hold public office. And "I know all I need to know" should be a confession that one leads a simple life, consisting of eating, sleeping, shitting, masturbating, and watching sports on TV. Instead, it's become the battle cry of the American idiot based on the assumption that fancy book learnin' is less legitimate than the deeper, folksy wisdom one acquires from milking cows. Think I'm exaggerating? Check out a book that recently made it to the Top Ten of *The New York Times* Best Seller list.

In October 2014, former Arkansas preacher/governor, and perennial losing presidential candidate Mike Huckabee released his "heads up, I'm runnin' again!" book, entitled: *God, Guns, Grits, and Gravy*. Now, of course it's possible it only made the Best Seller list because Huck's folks bought up a whole mess of copies to create the illusion that people thought he had something important to say. You know, like they did with Sarah Palin's book. Nevertheless, there are problems with the book, and Huck's theory.

First: the title, which is based on the notion that there's a God who created an entire universe, yet who has a super special place in his heart for fat, heavily armed Christians with high cholesterol. Second: the notion that folks in the flyover states possess a simple, yet superior down home wisdom that we big city elitists with our fancy educations just don't get. I thought it was oily fish and blueberries that were brain food, not corn meal with goop poured over it. And last, it's a book. And Huck's people don't read books. They burn them. Only liberals and socialists read books. He should have dropped it as a country song. He could've played bass on the track.

And let's not forget another two-time presidential aspirant, Rick Santorum, who said: "The middle class? Since when in America do we have classes? That's Marxism talk." He also said, addressing a 2012 Values Voters Summit: "we will never have the elite, smart people on our side." (Yes, I know he's from Pennsylvania, a blue state. But he was born in Virginia.) Santorum also came out in opposition to early childhood education, warning that programs that put children in school as soon as possible were ploys for socialists to "take your children from the womb so they can indoctrinate them." He then added: "socialists love children." The fact is socialists don't love children any more or less than capitalists, communists, or anarchists. As more of a democratic socialist, and father of four, I find that sometimes I love my children, and other times I'm in agreement with W.C. Fields that I like them fine when they're properly cooked.

Then there's Aaron Osmond, of the singing Osmonds. The Osmonds were a popular '70s family musical group who were grown in a jar of mayonnaise. A Utah state representative from the 10th District, Osmond has called for an end to mandatory education.

Don't get me wrong -- I've met some nice Southern Republicans -- intelligent, good-hearted, well-meaning people, sincere in what they think. Not that I'd want my sister to marry one. But to the extent that they pine for a simpler time, embrace traditional values like hard work, decency, and family they're just fine. To the extent that they're paranoid racist assholes, they're not. And neither are their rich counterparts -- those pasty, Rosacea-faced, bulbous-nosed alcoholics in their pastel blazers who stink of privilege as they knock back dry martinis in their restricted country clubs, while whispering ethnic jokes out of earshot of the Mexican bartender, while their desiccated, cotton candy-haired wives get quietly hammered in the corner and secretly pine for someone to touch them, even the Mexican bartender. They're all relics of a mythical era called the good old days, the '50s, or the Reagan years.

So, is it unfair and prejudicial to claim that the most conservative red states are the dumbest, fattest, drunkest, poorest, sickest, and most heavily armed in the country, and that their beliefs, voting habits and elected representatives are screwing up life for the rest of us? No, it's not, because they are.

According to a 2014 *Huffington Post* article, Southern states are consistently behind the rest of the country in wages, economic mobility, education, and health care. However, they lead the country in incest, teen pregnancy, gun deaths, incarceration, poverty, obesity, intoxication, and general unhappiness. They're also still hooked on creationism, and freaked out over gay marriage. It's like evolution took a detour, crashed through a dead end sign and plunged into a swamp. But instead of calling for help, it mated with the swamp creatures and built a civilization. But don't take my word for it. Let's look at some stats.

THE 10 REDDEST STATES

Arkansas, South Carolina, North Dakota, Louisiana, South Dakota, Utah, Wyoming, Alabama, Idaho, Mississippi. As of 2014, Republican lawmakers from those states outnumbered Democrats 15-5 in the Senate and 55-16 in the House. Most of the members of the House Freedom Caucus are from red states. The governors of these states are Republicans. And the GOP has a majority in their state legislatures.

THE 10 DUMBEST STATES

Georgia, Tennessee, Hawaii, Alabama, Alaska, Louisiana, California, Nevada, New Mexico, Mississippi, Arizona. (9 red or reddish. 1 blue. Yes, California's on the list, but that's just 'cause the dumber parts bring down the curve.)

Three red state presidential candidates in the 2012 election advocated abolishing the Department of Education: Ron Paul (R-Texas), Newt Gingrich (R-Georgia), and Rick "Oops" Perry (R-Texas.) In 2015, Senator Ted Cruz (R-Texas) re-enacted Perry's debate brain fart when he couldn't remember the fifth of the five government agencies he'd get rid of. A trip to his website provided the missing agency: the Department of Education. Why? Because they don't want the smarty-pants federal government coming down and telling them they can't teach a fairy tale about the origins of the universe.

In Texas, the state panel responsible for selecting high school biology textbooks includes a nutritionist who believes in "creation science," and a chemical engineer who is a "Darwin skeptic."

In June 2015, Texas Governor Greg Abbott named a homeschooler to chair the State Board of Education. Texas also allowed school textbooks to state that Moses inspired the Constitution.

In South Carolina, a state senator has blocked evolution from the school science standards. A Louisiana state representative wants the Bible to be the state book. An Alabama education official issued a warning about a "homosexualist Common Core takeover of education in Southern states."

A Louisiana institution called The Discovery Institute, which refers to itself, completely without irony, as a "creationist think tank," writes and supplies supplemental textbooks to schools that wish to teach creationism. They also helped write a bill called The Louisiana Science Education Act of 2008, which opened the door for allowing creationist materials inside the classroom. A similar law exists in Tennessee.

Private and publicly funded charter schools in Arizona, Arkansas, Florida, Georgia, Louisiana, Texas, and Utah are allowed to teach creationism as a valid, alternative theory to evolution. Colorado, Missouri, Montana, and Oklahoma have bills allowing students to be taught creationism. They're disguised as measures promoting academic freedom but can be recognized by their official name: The Imbecile Protection Act. Indiana, South Carolina, Kansas, and Kentucky have advocated teaching creationism alongside evolution.

Thanks to an emphasis on abstinence-only sex education, nine of the ten states with the highest rates of teen pregnancy are red states. In Mississippi, the sex education curriculum teaches students that homosexuality is illegal.

In Augusta County, Virginia, a teacher handed out a homework assignment on Islam, which asked students to copy the Islamic statement of faith – the *Shahada* – to give them an appreciation of Arabic calligraphy. The uproar was instantaneous, with many parents decrying it as an attempt to convert their children to Islam, and calling for the teacher's firing. As a precautionary measure, every school in the district was closed the following day. The assignment came from a standard workbook on world religions.

A school board in Coeur d'Alene, Idaho considered banning Nobel prize-winning author John Steinbeck's *Of Mice and Men* from high school classrooms. According to a school board trustee: "There's just too darn much cussing…" Of course, the Bible's ok. Even with the story about the guy who gets stuck on wooden boards, and has nails slammed into his hands and feet. That story gets a pass. I guess the lesson is that violence is ok, just as long as there's no cussin' in it. Like you wouldn't be cussin' if someone slammed nails into you.

The word "education" is from the Latin *educo*, meaning to lead out. Like from the darkness of ignorance into the light of knowledge. The U.S. has the most prestigious schools in the world. Harvard University was founded in 1636, with the motto *veritas*: Latin, for truth. Yale University was founded in 1701 with the motto *lux et veritas*: light and truth. Even the fictional Faber College from *Animal House* was founded in 1904 under the motto *Knowledge is Good*. Then there's Liberty University, founded by the late, hardly lamented Jerry Falwell. Their motto: *Training Champions for Christ since 1971*.

Here's the thing: if you're going to walk the Earth with that accent, so that every time you open your mouth that drawly shitkicker twang drips out like gravy rollin' down a fat guy's chin, you might at least try to counteract it with some danged intelligence. As a carrier of a nasally Long Island, New York accent, I will never be mistaken in the dark for a member of the British aristocracy. But at least I've done my darnedest over the years to take the curse off the accent with some fancy book learnin'.

THE 10 FATTEST STATES

Mississippi, West Virginia, Delaware, Louisiana, Arkansas, South Carolina, Tennessee, Ohio, Kentucky, Oklahoma. (8 red, 2 blue)

A 2015 Gallup study revealed that, as fat as we are, we're getting fatter. National obesity increased from 26.2% in 2012, to 27.1% in 2013, to nearly 28% in 2015. That means over 1 in 4 Americans is fat. So, if you're having breakfast at

Denny's with three other people, and you don't see the fatty -- it's you -- and probably the waitress, the cook, the dishwasher, the hostess, and the cashier. The study also noted that the average American is now 23 pounds heavier than his or her ideal body weight. Imagine walking around with a 23-pound weight all day. Who would do that, other than a mom with a fat kid in a snuggly?

Yet, these stats should hardly be surprising, given the menu items at some of our most popular chain restaurants. There's Burger King's *Large Triple Whopper with Fries and Cheese* maxing out at a death-defying 2110 calories. Or Wendy's *Hot and Juicy Triple with Cheese,* which tops out at a modest 1120. For sheer gluttony with a side of patriotism, there's Carl's Jr.'s 1030 calorie, 649 grams of fat, 2,350 mg. of sodium *Most American Thickburger* -- a half-pound Angus beef patty topped with Lay's Kettle Cooked Potato Chips, cheese, pickles, onion, ketchup, mustard, and... wait for it... a split hot dog, all on a fresh bun. At this point, they might as well throw in a can of Bud, a tin of Skoal, and a Slim Jim. The commercial features a *Sports Illustrated* swimsuit model eating the burger in a hot tub, with the voice over: "*The American Thickburger. Why? Because America. That's why!*" And for the pork-lover, there's Applebee's new *Triple Hog Dare Ya,* featuring pulled pork, Black Forest ham, thick-sliced bacon, crispy onions, and melted cheddar on a ciabatta roll: 1140 calories, 62 g. fat, 2640 mg. sodium, and 125 mg. cholesterol. It also comes with unlimited fries. And for desert the cook comes to your table and punches you in the heart.

And let's not forget KFC's *Double Down* -- two pieces of fried chicken, bacon, cheese, and mayo, with the fried chicken replacing the bun. KFC serves their food in a bucket. How much clearer do they have to be that they think their customers are animals? Do they actually have to dump it in a trough or toss it on the ground like chicken feed? But, they've been in business for over sixty years so I guess someone's eating it. I had it once, forty years ago, and I think I'm still crapping it out.

And which states spend the most on fast food? Alabama, Kentucky, Louisiana, Maryland, Mississippi, Ohio, Oklahoma, Texas, Utah, and West Virginia. (8 red, 2 blue.)

Mississippi, a leader in the dumb category, has also recently risen to the top of the fat list. As of 2013, 35.4% of Mississippians were obese, taking the crown from West Virginia, which held it from 2010-2012. They spend about 62% of their dining out budget on fast food. Its victory has also been attributed to, in no small part, the passage of the anti-Bloomberg bill, which prevents government from limiting how much its citizens can eat or drink. It takes a particularly astute level of political sophistication to conflate the founding fathers' struggle for freedom with the right to guzzle mass quantities of colored sugar water. Give me Mountain Dew, or give me death!

Alabama spends 60% of their dining out budget on fast food. More than 66% of the population is overweight. Heart disease and diabetes are sky high. Kentucky boasts the country's 2nd highest obesity rate. It's also the home of KFC.

It must be the reason their state bird is the fried chicken. In *Men's Health* magazine's annual list of fattest U.S. cities, Texas cities accounted for half. Guess the South's not going to rise again. Though if it does, it's going to take a crane to hoist its 600-pound ass off the couch.

And let's not forget the fat kids. Childhood obesity in the U.S. has more than tripled over the last 30 years. A 2013 report entitled *F as in Fat* revealed the seven states with the highest childhood obesity rates: Mississippi, South Carolina, Louisiana, Tennessee, Arkansas, Arizona, and Kentucky. (All red.)

Projected gross revenue for the fast food industry in 2015 is $709 billion. Instead of firing drones at the terrorists, maybe we should just airdrop a *Triple Hog Dare Ya*.

THE 10 SICKEST STATES

Mississippi, Arkansas, Louisiana, Kentucky, Oklahoma, Tennessee, West Virginia, Alabama, South Carolina, and Indiana. (10 red, no blue.)

Taking the number one spot as the least healthy state, Mississippi boasts the second-lowest rate of doctors and dentists. Not surprisingly, the fat states also had the highest rates of chronic disease, high blood pressure, high cholesterol, diabetes, cancer, heart attacks, and depression. They also excel in premature death and infant mortality, teen pregnancy, smoking, lack of exercise, low vaccination rates, low vegetable consumption, abortion rates, and STDs.

South Carolina has high rates of salmonella and chlamydia. So if you find yourself in Greenville with a sudden craving for steak tartare and a blow job -- leave.

THE 10 POOREST STATES

Mississippi, Arkansas, Tennessee, West Virginia, Louisiana, Montana, South Carolina, Kentucky, Alabama, and North Carolina. (10 red, no blue. Other articles on the subject include New Mexico and Georgia among the top 10. Both red.)

A 2014 article on *The Huffington Post* referred to the South as a grim block of poverty. Over 30% of Southerners live below the federal poverty line. Guess they're just too fat to jump over it. Kentucky takes the prize. Nearly 32% of their children live in poverty, the worst rate in the nation. The South also boasts the lowest wages, and lowest economic mobility.

THE TEN MOST HEAVILY ARMED STATES

Kentucky, Utah, Montana, Wyoming, Alaska, West Virginia, South Dakota, North Dakota, Arkansas and Alabama. (10 red, no blue.)

Number 11 on the list is Tennessee, where the governor signed a bill in

2015 allowing gun owners with permits to bring their weapons to state and local parks. Advocates of the bill said it would improve park safety. Jack Daniels is made in Lynchburg, Tennessee. Whiskey and guns, sounds like a recipe for safety.

In December 2015, Liberty University, where they've been training champions for Christ since 1971, formally ended a ban on guns in dormitories. According to University president Jerry Falwell, Jr., "The move is aimed at keeping the Virginia campus safe from terrorist attacks." He then added "Let's teach them a lesson if they ever show up here." Yes, I'm sure Liberty U. is high on the list of ISIS hard targets. Right after Dollywood, Branson, and Ken Ham's Creation Museum.

THE TEN MOST RELIGIOUS STATES

Mississippi, Utah, Alabama, Louisiana, Arkansas, South Carolina, Tennessee, North Carolina, Georgia, Oklahoma. (10 red, no blue.)

You'd think all that God-fearin' would lead to a better quality of life. But according to a study by a University of Chicago law professor who examined life in our most religious states, they rank among the worst in the nation in citizens living below the poverty line, obesity, overall health, rate of incarceration, smoking, life expectancy, and gun deaths.

80% of their senators are Republicans. 57% of Republicans want to dismantle the Constitution and make Christianity the national religion.

Coincidentally, the most religious states in the country also watch the most porn. 'Cause, as we know, the human libido won't flare up if you beat it down with a Bible. Maybe all that porn-watching comes from *Genesis 1:28*, where God said to "be fruitful and watch other people pretend to multiply."

THE 10 MOST DEPRESSED STATES

Arkansas, Indiana, Kentucky, Michigan, Mississippi, Missouri, Nevada, Oklahoma, Tennessee, West Virginia. The reason for their citizens' depression? They live there. Across the board, red states are at the bottom of the pack in education, obesity, sickness, and poverty. Yet, many individual states have also managed to excel in their own unique areas.

MOST RACIST TWEETS
Alabama.

MOST UFO SIGHTINGS
Arizona.

MOST HATE GROUPS
Arkansas.

MOST REGISTERED SEX OFFENDERS
Delaware.

MOST PORNOGRAPHY PAGES VIEWS
Kansas.

MOST SMOKERS AND HIGHEST CANCER RATES
Kentucky.

MOST PEOPLE IN PRISON
Louisiana.

MOST METH LAB INCIDENTS
Missouri.

HIGHEST RATES OF MENTAL ILLNESS
New Mexico.

MOST EXECUTIONS
Oklahoma.

MOST MEGACHURCHES
Tennessee.

During the 2012 primaries, Rick Perry floated the notion of secession. And while he never literally went on record supporting it, a petition in Texas in favor of bugging out of the U.S. received 50,000 signatures. According to *Yahoo News*, after the 2012 election, 69 separate petitions for secession, with more than 675,000 names, were submitted to the White House. In 2013, 125,000 Texans sent a similar letter demanding that Texas be allowed to secede. During the 2014 midterms a poll was taken asking if people were so fed up with government that they'd be willing to have their state secede. One out of four said they would, including 53% of Tea Party members.

So, here's the thing: if Texas, or, for that matter, any other red state is of a mind to break off from the U.S. and go on their own, my attitude is: GO! GET THE FUCK OUT! Unlike during the Civil War, we won't come after you.

You can actually draw a pretty clean line from Texas, west to Florida, north to North Carolina, west through Kentucky, Indiana, and Missouri, north to North Dakota, west through Idaho, then back down through Utah to Arizona, then west through New Mexico and back to Texas. The shit breaks off real clean. Maybe you can frack the borders so the whole chunk will snap off and drift down into the Gulf of Mexico. Or if that's not geologically feasible, just stay put and we'll build a fence. Or a great wall with Trump's picture on it. Might work. If I saw that asshole's fat face at the border, I'd turn around. You don't want anybody to fence you in? Fine. We'll fence you out. Either way you can take your God, guns, grits and gravy and go New Testament batshit crazy together. Set it up like one of those old west towns you seem to pine for. You won't even need to hold elections. You've already got the folks to run it.

Rick Perry as Mayor. Hannity as Sheriff. Ted Nugent as his bumbling deputy. O'Reilly as the gunslinger with the reputation for shooting men in the back. Ted Cruz as the shady gambler with a derringer in his boot. Limbaugh as the sadistic cattle rancher. Steve Doocy as the town drunk. Santorum as the fire and brimstone preacher. Palin as the schoolmarm. Trump as the wealthy railroad baron who secretly likes to dress in lingerie and have the whores whip him. And as for the cadres of Murdoch's fembots; well, I guess someone's got to snap those whips. I'm sure Megyn Kelly would be more than happy to take a crack at it.

You can even take the national anthem. It's a grating, unsingable song. We'll get John Legend or Stevie Wonder to pen something with some soul. You can also make a new flag. Maybe the Confederate Stars and Bars, with a bald eagle clutching a Bushmaster in one claw, a can of Bud in the other, and an unfiltered Camel sticking out of its mouth. Call the country whatever you like: Assholia. Christy-land. Or Alabama. We don't care. Just get out. Although, if you could, leave Austin. I hear it's a cool place. And Sedona. Oh, and we'll also hang on to New Orleans. And Memphis. And Nashville. And Miami. And Atlanta.

And as for the people who live in red states who don't think like the rest of you, they can stay here in America. We'll grant them political/mental asylum. Then we'll seal off the border with a Disneyland-style sign at the checkpoint reading: you must be this intelligent to live in Smart America.

But if you don't leave, and we're stuck together, can you do the rest of us a favor? Smarten up, and join the 21st century. The old South is dead and it's never gonna rise again. And let go of the confederate flag. It's like you're holding up a sign advertising "150 years of racism and proud of it!" Look, I did some bad shit in my life but I try to sort it out, and get to the root of what might have been driving me, psychologically. I don't brag about it on a bumper sticker.

And give up the Bible obsession. It's just a dusty old book written thousands of years ago. It's not a science book, or a sex manual. And while it does contain a few decent lessons in morality, there's also a lot of stoning in it. See if you can set a spell and try to sort out the different parts. And while you're at it, crack a few other books. We've got some real good ones, many written by people from your neck of the woods.

Also, stop electing mutts to government. Like state representative Bill Chumley, from South Carolina's District 35, covering Greenville and Spartanburg counties. Chumley told CNN that the problem with the victims in the Charleston church shooting was that it was like they were just waiting for their turn to be shot. He then added, "somebody in there with a means of self-defense could've stopped this." Yeah, that's the problem in this country -- not enough guns in church.

You've got smart people down there. Elect them, so they can represent you. Because the way things are, the dumb ones are really screwing up life for everyone else. It would be one thing if they just stayed dumb privately, but the problem is they vote. And at the end of the day, a dumbed-down population is also a dumbed-down electorate.

CHAPTER SEVEN

DUMBF✯CK POLITICS

DISINFORMATION NATION

"A lie can travel halfway around the world before the truth can put its pants on." Mark Twain

Newton's Third Law of Motion states that for every action there is an equal and opposite reaction. Just as post-Civil War Reconstruction gave rise to the KKK and John Birch Society, Barack Obama's 2008 victory over Grandpa Munster and his ditzy night nurse kicked off a right wing freak-out. JFK's declaration in his 1960 inaugural address that "the torch has been passed to a new generation" was a beacon of hope for the future. This inaugural torch was picked up by a mob of angry villagers and they rampaged into town shrieking about socialism.

The Republican freak-out played out on two levels. Prior to the election, the only thing that got your old-school racist's ass out of the trailer in the morning was the feeling that, no matter how fat, dumb, or poor he may be, at least he was white and, therefore, better off. But when a Harvard-educated black guy gets elected President, that rationalization is rendered inoperative. So, when they started shrieking about wanting their country back, what they meant was they wanted the last, fleeting remnant of their superiority back. That's racism on the micro level.

On the macro level, the election of Barack Obama meant that the GOP had to digest a new political reality: the electorate was changing. And it wasn't getting whiter. 95% of African Americans voted for Obama, as did 67% of Hispanics, and 62% of Asian Americans. That's a whole lot of change. And if there's one thing the old guard doesn't like, it's change, particularly when it could bring about the death of the Republican brand. Because the worst thing you can call a Democrat is inconsistent in his or her position or, horror of horrors, a hypocrite. The worst thing you can call a Republican is out of power. And they will say or do damn near anything to get it back.

Beginning inauguration day, with Dick Cheney tooling around in a wheelchair doing his best Dr. Strangelove impression, their single goal was to bring this president down by any means possible; to turn him into Welcome Back Carter instead of the Second Coming of Clinton. (No double entendre intended. Make your own joke if you absolutely must.) Mitch McConnell publically expressed this when he said, "The single most important thing we want to achieve is for President Obama to be a one-term president."

You could call their strategy Operation Monkeyshit. Just like a zoo chimp will wildly throw his poop at tourists, Republicans starting flinging everything they could get their hands on. Suddenly every GOP hack, flack and talking head began referring to the Democratic Party as the "Democrat" party. (A term also favored by the late, and one would think, unlamented Joe McCarthy.) Why? First, it sounds less democratic. Second, it sounds harsh, especially the "rat" part. This was just one of the Frank Luntz-style phrases that oozed from the mouths of Republicans. They also referred to the president as "this president" or "Barack Obama." Rarely, if ever, was he called President Obama, because that would confer legitimacy on someone they were desperately trying to delegitimize.

Legislatively, they took on the role of obstructionists, attempting to block this *arriviste* at every turn. This tactic that was confirmed by retired Republican Congressman, George Voinovich, who admitted they were told they could never give this president a victory. If Obama was for it, they had to be against it. And they were.

One has to give them credit for marching in lockstep, and calling cadence like good little soldiers. There was the "scrap the bill/start over" mantra, trotted out during the debates over health care reform; the "America doesn't have a revenue problem, it has a spending problem" and "don't raise taxes on anyone during a down economy" refrains used during the budget fights; the "Obama is leading from behind" attack during the Libyan uprising; and more recently the "let the American people decide" talking point in the fight over confirming Scalia's successor on the Supreme Court. Republicans harmonize so well you'd think they were the Gay Men's Choir.

In 2014, a ridiculously amateurish spot began appearing on MSNBC, citing crimes by the president and calling for his impeachment. Obviously, the people who paid for the ad knew they weren't going to impeach him. But say "impeachment" often enough and it will slowly seep into the average (dumb) voter's mind that the president must be doing something unlawful and therefore doesn't deserve to hold office. Then there were the threats to shut down the government, claiming it's non-functional. Sort of like sticking a plug in the ass of government, then bitching that it's constipated.

They also dusted off the old Clinton hatred, which was essentially the re-tooled FDR hatred. When Roosevelt was pushing the New Deal he was attacked by Republicans and rich industrialists for being a dictator, encouraging class warfare, and defying the Constitution. Sound familiar? Think of all the accusations that have been hurled at this president:

He's taking your freedom!

He's a foreigner!

He's going to take your guns!

He's housing terrorists in your neighborhood!

He's setting up death panels!

He's letting immigrant babies into the country!

He's making war on the rich!

He's making war on religion!

He's making war on Christmas!

He's a socialist!

He's a communist!

He's a fascist!

He's a Muslim!

He's a tyrant!

He's the worst president in history!

Legislative obstruction. Character assassination. All to create the narrative that his election was an aberration; a mistake that needed to be corrected. It was about tonnage, death by a thousand insults. Fact-based or not. Reality-based or not. It wasn't about the words. It was about the music. Only with President Obama they had an extra weapon: the old Southern strategy, 21st century style, based on the knowledge that they could tap into the dark side of the American psyche and play on the lingering cells of race hate still lurking in the body politic. Because, over time, all those insults go into the blender and liquefy into the one word they mean but know they can't say. Then with the conversation over health care reform, they had an actual battle to fight; hence, the Tea Party.

Here's the thing: if it's 1776 and you wake up, put on a tri-corner hat, grab a musket and head out to the public square to fight for freedom, you're a patriot. If it's 2009 and you do the same thing, you're an imbecile. The Tea Party was a sham – the illusion of a grass roots movement, concocted by The Koch Brothers and Dick Armey and his folks at FreedomWorks, and fobbed off as a populist uprising, with the president as the 21st century King George.

Think back to 2009 and the beginning of the debates over health care. Or as it was quickly demonized: OBAMACARE! Which was just a catchy name for what they really wanted to call it: THE SCARY BLACK RADICAL IS GOING TO KILL GRANDMA AND DESTROY AMERICA WITH SOCIALIZED MEDICINE ACT! Nevertheless, the term quickly weaseled its way into the American lexicon.

Remember the "town hall protesters," who suddenly seemed so outraged over the prospect of better health care that they jumped on their Rascal scooters and motored down to the local Elks Lodge to raise some patriotic hell? Given the collection of fat bastards who invaded those meetings, they should have called themselves The Future Diabetics of America. But it was fake outrage. The illusion of dissent, cooked up for its optical value.

As for the quality of the debate, when their elected representative tried to discuss the issue, their only contribution was to raise a thumbs-down, and yell, "boo!" Boo? If your intention is to roll into a public forum and demonstrate that you are possessed of a bovine mentality, why not just drop the pretense and yell, "moo"? You could glean their profound understanding of the issues from the early Tea Party signs, warning: "Keep your government hands off my Medicare!"

This was pure hype, a public relations stunt, spoon-fed to the country via Fox News, and swallowed whole by an uncritical media. It didn't take long before the nightly news shows featured stories about the town hall protestors. Even if the occasional broadcast included the modifier "so-called," it was the exception. I imagine, at one point, the folks at FreedomWorks sat in front of their TVs like Albert Brooks in *Broadcast News*, musing: "We say it here, and it comes out there."

But it accomplished its task by tarnishing the Affordable Care Act as a government takeover of our health care system. It also put two quick bullets in the head of the public option and single-payer, which were branded as socialized medicine, and relegated to the level of non-starter. And the evidence for the human devastation caused by socialized medicine? All those dead bodies piling up in England and Canada.

Then, once the law was passed, there was the effort to repeal. A TV spot that ran for years featured a voice over by Mike Huckabee, whose ominous tone was reminiscent of Vincent Price in Michael Jackson's "Thriller" video:

> *"In locked back rooms in the middle of the night,*
> *Obamacare was passed and*
> *rammed down the throat of the American people..."*

This spot ran almost daily on MSNBC, though I couldn't figure out the marketing strategy. Were they trying to stick a thumb in the eye of the liberal media? They certainly weren't swaying me to their position. After several years of pounding this notion into the conversation, Republicans began to cite a poll that stated that 53% of Americans were against the law. Of course they were. If you bombard the public with same ad ten times a day, then take a poll, the results are going to reflect the message in the ad. Then the reporting of the poll results becomes news. It's information alchemy, turning bullshit into facts.

Of course, these histrionic tactics are hardly new. Even as a tactic against health care. Go on YouTube and check out a 1961 recording entitled: *Ronald Reagan Speaks Out Against Socialized Medicine*. The subject was Medicare. Then private citizen Reagan warned:

> *"One of the traditional methods of imposing 'statism'*
> *or socialism on a people has been by way of medicine.*
> *It's very easy to disguise a medical program*
> *as a humanitarian project. Most people are a*
> *little reluctant to oppose anything that*
> *suggests medical care for people who possibly can't afford it."*

Sponsored by the American Medical Association, the recording goes on for over ten minutes. Reagan decried Medicare as the foot in the door for socialized medicine. Medicare and Medicare passed in 1965. Fifty years later, even after the Affordable Care Act passed, and then survived a tsunami of Republican opposition and legal challenges, still no socialized medicine. No socialism. No communism. No jack-booted thugs breaking down the door in the middle of the night to force grandma to sign a DNR.

More recently the Huckabee ads were revised, starring Dr. Ben Carson. For one brief, shining moment, Carson was the GOP's great black hope. In the ad, he called Obamacare "the worst thing since slavery." Really. Providing increased access to health care to millions of Americans is worse than putting

10.7 million people in bondage over a 350-year period. I assume Dr. Carson meant this metaphorically, in the sense that any kind of unearned health care amounts to an entitlement and weakens people, making them dependent on government handouts.

Maybe he has a point. And since he brought up slavery, based on his logic, 10.7 million Africans got free, unearned boat passage to the U.S. Instead of their descendants asking for reparations, maybe they should have to pay back the government for the trip, with interest. And they got free citizenship. (Ok, 3/5ths citizenship at first, but the other 2/5ths got there eventually, so I suppose those payments could be pro-rated.) And all it took was centuries of unimaginable human suffering and degradation, 620,000 people dying in the Civil War, and then another 100 years until the civil rights movement. But it got there. So, pay up, black people. The free ride is over.

Then there was the "birther" nonsense, spearheaded by Trump, as a way of firmly establishing his credentials as a flaming asshole who would say anything for personal or political gain. This ratfuck of a stunt actually gained so much traction it lead to the president revealing his Hawaiian birth certificate to quell the noise, the way you stick a bottle in the mouth of a screaming infant to shut it up. But they still weren't satisfied, as the right floated out the insane rumor that it was a forgery.

Think back to April 2011, and the first time the Donald ran for president. Although he was called out by Lawrence O'Donnell, who stated that Trump's campaign was nothing more than a PR stunt to hawk his reality show, Trump persisted in his lie. Appearing on *The Today Show* and referring to the President's birth certificate, he stated, with his usual bullshit bravado, that he had researchers on the ground in Hawaii who "cannot believe what they are finding!" He backed this up with the accusation that Obama's grandmother said she witnessed her grandson's birth – in Kenya. Sadly, the interviewer never pressed the matter, which was not surprising, since Trump's show was also on NBC. Truth will always take a back seat to corporate synergy.

That was in 2011. By late 2014, no evidence had been offered by Trump or his investigators. If they had actually found something, it would have been the scandal of the century and nothing would have stopped Trump's bloated ego from taking it public. But he didn't, because there was nothing there. Yet, in early 2015, he was back on the campaign trail whipping it up again. (He does know the president can't run for a third term? Perhaps someone should tell him.) Even in late 2015, when asked by Chris Matthews if he would finally admit that the president is a U.S. citizen, Trump adamantly refused to answer the question. This was his snarky way of keeping the lie floating in the air without actually having to admit that he was lying.

Yet, every time this subject would raise its pointed head, the left would utter the plaintive cry, "He's shown them his birth certificate, what more do they want?!" The answer is simple: they didn't want anything. Again, it wasn't the words. It was the music. The birther non-story was just another note in the dog whistle symphony they were playing, the ultimate goal of which was to turn Barack Obama into the Manchurian President.

Not that lies and negative ads are new in politics. In just the last 50 years we've had Nixon's dirty tricksters, Lee Atwater, and his spawn, Karl Rove. Think back to Bush 41's Willie Horton ads, Rove's hatchet job on Max Cleland during Cleland's 2002 campaign to defend his Senate seat. Then there was the rumor about John McCain's secret black child, a sinister allegation that wafted out of the Bush camp during the 2000 Republican primaries and, of course, John Kerry's swiftboating.

Though it's not like Democrats haven't been known to hit hard, as with the classic 1968 Daisy Girl spot, which painted Barry Goldwater as nuke happy. Considering Goldwater did advocate nuking Vietnam, the ads did have some basis in fact. Nevertheless, the spot ended with an explosion, and mushroom cloud -- the go-to image for painting your opponent as being hell-bent on Armageddon.

And if negative ads don't work, try scandal, or the appearance of scandal. The ultimate lesson of Watergate was not that we should clean up our act. It was that a scandal could bring down a president. Or at least seize the narrative and force him off his game. And if there's no actual scandal, just make one up. As Orson Wells' character in *Citizen Kane* cabled his reporter, "You provide the prose poems, I'll provide the war." It's just a matter of tossing out allegations and forcing your opponent to respond, or face media cries of, "Does their silence mean they're hiding something?" It's guilt by accusation. The political equivalent of "when did you stop beating your wife." This was the weapon of choice against Bill Clinton. Troopergate. Nannygate. Commercegate. Travelgate. Whitewater. Vince Foster. They just kept up the barrage until they were eventually handed a juicy story on a platter.

Subsequent attacks against President Obama involved three pseudo-scandals: IRS, Fast and Furious, and Benghazi. At one point, it simply became a matter of repeating these buzz words so that they took on an evil all their own. There was a moment in 2014 when John Boehner stopped to talk to reporters and, in all his leathery glory, robotically blurted, "Benghazi, IRS, Fast and Furious. The American people deserve to know the truth." He recited the talking points then most likely went off to play 18 holes, and suck down a few Scotches in the clubhouse. (Given the relentless pressure put on him by the extreme right wing of his party, I'm guessing he needed them.)

And if a scandal has legs, there's always the special prosecutor or congressional investigation. Subpoena high-ranking government officials and vilify them on camera, hoping they'll trip up under the pressure or, in the best of all possible words, lie. Then you've got them for perjury. Instant headlines. End of political career.

Darrell Issa's 2014 House Oversight and Government Reform Committee dragged in then Secretary of State Hillary Clinton to testify about Benghazi. But for all the posturing and grandstanding, none of it was about uncovering the truth. It was about creating the illusion of lies and a cover-up, and damaging the administration. The medium is the message. Because deep down we think where there's smoke there's fire. If someone's testifying before Congress, they must have done something wrong. And if someone on the committee should try to bring some sanity to the proceedings, like Representative John Lewis did, just cut off his mike, because that's democracy.

Negative ads, talking points, and investigations -- all weapons in a disinformation campaign. And they work. They work because we're stupid and because the news doesn't call them out on it, because the news is no longer The News. Even though the network Evening News shows play to between 7-9 million people, they no longer have the same influence. They're almost a sad anachronism, given that, by the time they air, they're basically highlights of information we've read all day online.

The upside of news decentralization is that it removes corporations as the sole gatekeepers of information. The downside is that we all stand inside our echo chambers without any perspective from a trusted national figure who can act as ombudsman for truth. No Edward R. Murrow to take down Joe McCarthy. No Walter Cronkite to cast doubt on the government's whitewashed statements on the Vietnam War. No Dan Rather to get in Nixon's face. The Brian Williams fiasco at NBC was the dagger in the heart of the trusted network news anchor.

Not that these broadcasts aim for controversy. Given the ratings pressure they're under, they very often bend over backwards to display equanimity but, in doing so, end up providing a platform for candidates or spokespersons to throw in talking points, unchallenged, so that interviews become virtual infomercials. It may seem like journalistic integrity, but it functions as self-neutering.

And when there's too much bad news, there's always the feel-good segment to take the curse off. During the Iraq War, news shows frequently ran the story about some soldier sneaking into his child's school for a surprise reunion. They still run from time to time. We're such suckers for the kid who erupts with shock and awe when he sees that daddy or mommy's home from the war. It was almost a daily spectacle during the holidays. And, yes, I get choked up when I see them. Who wouldn't? That's how powerful they are. But the emotion and tears of the reunion subtly legitimize the war, itself. It's the ultimate misdirection. After all, how could these noble people sacrifice so much for an ignoble cause.

Even the weekend chat shows seem to be designed for maximum noise and minimum analysis. They get the lefty and the righty on screen, throw the raw meat of the latest controversy in front of them, and watch them rip at each other. It's not a dialogue in the sense of an exchange of ideas intended to arrive at the truth. It's more of a talking points cage match. A clever trick you'll see when

Republicans appear on these shows is that they'll frown and shake their heads while their opponent's speaking, in order to pull focus and silently negate the point. Trump's been doing this during the Republican debates, though with him it's not a tactic. It's because he's an asshole.

No one's ever claimed politics is a gentleman's game. Power corrupts and the lust for power corrupts absolutely. It's always been about lies, double-crosses, electoral maps, political calculation, and psychological profiling of the electorate. Of finding the hot buttons and tailoring your message with dog-whistle language and buzz words that either fill simple folk with hope or stoke them with fear. The tactics used in political campaigns are a direct reflection of who we are as a people, and as an electorate.

We're inundated with political ads because we rarely question anything that comes out of the box. Given the notion of worship that's built into our view of religion, it's no miracle that the TV has become our in-house pulpit. We watch it, passively. No one ever thinks to ask who's paying for these spots. And why? *Cui bono?* Who benefits? Who's got the kind of money to fund an effort like this and why are they doing it?

Lincoln's declaration: "You can fool all of the people some of the time, and some of the people all the time, but you cannot fool all the people all the time" may have once carried some weight. But you no longer have to fool all the people all the time. You just have to fool enough of them, at a particular time, in particular states or congressional districts by pushing their buttons with cleverly designed ads to sway them on Election Day. When Rove pushed the "married gays will move next door and homosexualize your children" button in Ohio in 2004, it brought home George Bush's re-election.

Campaign managers know that the voters are malleable, their fears and prejudices playable. If they weren't dumb, the effect of political advertising would be minimal. I've never seen a 30-second political spot in my life that I gave any credence to. Either for a candidate I supported, or one I didn't. I assume most every ad is filled with half-truths, propaganda, and lies.

For all the platitudes about respecting and informing the American voter, those whose job it is to advise political campaigns rely almost exclusively on our susceptibility to messages that come out of the box, whether it's via commercials, or political talk shows. When Bill Maher busts Fox News in a lie, it's a gotcha moment -- to anyone who reads books and ties their own shoelaces. But not to Fox, because they're not in the truth game. When Fox is busted in a lie, they simply tell a new one, or tell the same one in a different way. They're impervious to facts. Or satire. They know they're lying. They just don't care. A 2015 report from Punditfact – a partnership between *The Tampa Bay Times* and *Politifact.com* – stated that 60% of the facts reported by Fox were false. And I'm sure Roger Ailes isn't losing sleep over it.

(I always imagine the morning editorial meeting at Fox News is Ailes as Jabba the Hut, holding leashes on their gaggle of fembots wearing gold chain bikinis and choke collars, with Steve Doocy, cackling like that rodent, and Murdoch's face on the Jumbotron. I think Ailes has the same fantasy, only with the president encased in Carbonite.)

The political atmosphere has been polluted by what Steven Colbert referred to as "Truthiness." To that, I would add the term "factitious." Lies that travel in via statistics, and cited by people who are confident that the public isn't smart enough to question a statement that's got a few numbers in it. Unless someone in the conversation knows enough to debunk the claim on the spot, it goes forth as truth. That's why many GOP spokespersons enter TV debates armed with two or three factitious statements, often citing some genuine-sounding patriotic source like The Heritage Foundation, The American Enterprise Institute, FreedomWorks, American Crossroads, Americans for Prosperity, The Cato Institute, Citizens for a Sound Economy, or Judicial Watch. The organizations sound beyond reproach. Why would anyone assume they're right wing lobbies and think tanks? Because if the talking head cited the latest research from the Selfish, Greedy Bastards Who Want to Keep Screwing You Blue Foundation, it might raise some skepticism even among the most trusting souls. We've been hit with a massive amount of disinformation over the last 7 years and no one in the media seems willing or able to play spot the lie. So, let's play:

THE LIE:
OBAMACARE!

The truth: the Affordable Care Act. Despite the fact that the law dealt in the insurance companies, the GOP launched a full-frontal assault against it out of fear that if it became as popular as Medicare or Medicaid, Democrats would ride that wave of approval and Republicans would continue their backwards march into oblivion. So, screw the uninsured. Screw the sick. Kill the bill. It was interesting that in the first wave of the assault, the same people who said the health care bill was 2000+ pages and impossible to read still knew they were against it.

Under the Affordable Care Act, nearly 14 million people have gotten coverage. A 2015 study by the Rand Corporation stated that every single thing Republicans said about the bill has turned out to be wrong: "It's a job killer." Wrong. Unemployment is 5%, the lowest it's been in 7 years. 75% of business owners said that ACA has not affected hiring practices. "It's all Medicaid expansion." Wrong. "It would stop employers from offering coverage." Wrong. The biggest gain in coverage was from employer-sponsored insurance.

In June 2015 the Supreme Court finally ruled in the case of *King v. Burwell*, brought by opponents of the law. The case hinged on a literal reading of four words. But those four words, if narrowly interpreted, could have gutted the federal exchanges and sent the law careening into a death spiral. Fortunately, for the millions whose health care was hanging in the balance, the court struck down the challenge.

Even Karl Rove has finally admitted that it's time to give it up. Yet, even though over 50 votes to repeal the law have failed, it's still Republican orthodoxy to get rid of it, although they don't offer up many specifics beyond that. In early 2016, George Stephanopoulos asked Trump how he'd replace the law, and the candidate burped, "we'll work something out." Perhaps he forgot the answer he gave CNN in July of 2015, when he said he'd replace it with "something terrific." Like what? Every cancer patient gets a lollypop?

Unless we elect a Republican president, the campaign to repeal the law will mostly likely fade away. The law will be amended, and fine-tuned, but will not disappear, which probably means we'll stop hearing the word Obamacare, because the same people who tried to kill it will want to strip the president's name off it once it's clearly working. Chances are they'll pivot back to Romneycare. (ROMNEY FOR PRESIDENT! 2020!)

THE LIE:
VOTER FRAUD!

The truth: The Republican freak-out over the changing national electorate gave rise to the Acorn scandal. And who uncovered this diabolical Democrat plot to register millions of illegal voters and subvert the electoral process: A couple of young, intrepid reporters, or some courageous whistleblower? No. It was a scrawny, opportunistic little culture warrior who went into mommy's closet and played pimp dress up with his girlfriend just to stage a make-pretend *60 Minutes* gotcha moment that was clearly more Mickey Mouse than Mike Wallace. Still, that didn't stop Fox from whipping it into a national frenzy.

Caucasians are projected to lose their majority status in the population by 2043. According to U.S. Census Bureau research, the non-Hispanic white population is projected to peak in 2024. The research also states that by 2016, Hispanics will represent 1 in 3 Americans, as opposed to 1 in 6. Can you say *El Presidente Vive en la Casa Blanca?* Because of this come to *Jesus* moment, an immediate effort had to be made to stop people from registering, by any means possible, and by any lie possible.

In 2008, Florida Governor Rick Scott went after the historically mendacious League of Women Voters by enacting a measure that would fine them $100,000 for registering an ineligible voter. Ironic that the state that swung the 2000 election to George Bush made accusations of voter fraud.

Since then, 14 states have passed voter ID laws: Alabama, Arkansas, Kansas, Mississippi, North Carolina, North Dakota, New Hampshire, Pennsylvania, Rhode Island, South Carolina, Tennessee, Texas, Virginia, and Wisconsin. The most insidious move has been in Alabama, which closed DMV offices in several predominantly African American counties, making it more difficult for people to get the very IDs they'd need to vote. More recently, the newly elected Tea Party governor of Kentucky issued an order removing voting rights from 140,000 former felons. Those affected were predominantly African-American. And all this has been made possible by a 2013 Supreme Court decision, gutting a key provision in the Voting Rights Act that prevented states from changing certain voting rules without prior federal approval.

For all the Trumped up fury against illegal immigrants raping and murdering Americans while taking their jobs away and putting a drain on the educational and health care systems, ultimately the GOP doesn't care how many Latinos slip into the country. They're not going to round up and deport over 11 million people. Here's the bottom line to Latinos: The Republican Party doesn't care if you stay. They just don't want you to vote.

There's a long history in this country of discriminatory regulations designed to stop certain people from voting. But as long as we're gutting the Voting Rights Act, we might as well bring back literacy tests, consisting of one simple question: Did God write the Constitution? If anyone answers "yes" their records are stamped TDTV -- Too Dumb To Vote.

THE LIE:
THE CLIMATE CHANGE DEBATE

The truth: there is no climate change debate. 97% of world's scientists agree that climate change is real, and is the result of human activity. And yet, in 2015, Senator James Inhofe, the same man who said that climate change isn't real, because God is in control of the world, appeared on the floor of the Senate with a snowball to prove that the climate isn't getting warmer. And no one threw him out. Or pelted him with the snowball. Or made him stand there and hold it for an hour to demonstrate the physical properties of water and how it freezes when subjected to cold, but then melts when subjected to heat. Or laughed his ass out of D.C. Someone needs to ask Inhofe if he was ever in New York or L.A. in the '70s, and if so, does he accept the fact that air pollution was the result of automobile emissions. We now have catalytic converters on cars and increased fuel efficiency standards, which the automotive industry fought for years. Now fuel efficiency is a selling point in car ads, though that's obviously more for economic reasons than ecological.

The Republican strategy against the reality of climate change has simply been a series of stall tactics to parry the relentless encroachment of facts. It's like we're living in the Monty Python Dead Parrot Sketch. In 2014, the talking point became, "I'm not a scientist so I can't say whether it's true or not." Right. And I'm not a doctor, but if I need surgery, I'm going to trust a doctor to do it. I don't have to be a doctor myself.

In August 2015, then presidential candidate Rick Santorum appeared on *Real Time with Bill Maher*, and when the subject came up, he floated out the mangled, factitious claim that: "The most recent survey of climate scientists said about 57% don't agree with the idea that 95% of the change in the climate is being caused by CO2." And while host and guest went back and forth in an "is not, is so" exchange, it couldn't be debunked in the moment. This is how lies worm their way into the national dialogue. Even though Maher negated the stat a week later, it did its job by polluting the conversation.

As the discussion continued, Santorum switched to the second line of defense, citing the economic devastation that would be caused by trying to fix the problem. This is the classic Republican two-step. Step one: It's definitely not happening. Step two: Even if it is happening, it would destroy the economy to fix it. This is no different from car manufacturers stonewalling on seat belts, sugar companies resisting regulations limiting the sugar content in products, or cigarette companies fighting health warnings on their packs. The tactics are always the same: Stall. Deny. Fight. Obstruct. Misinform. Misdirect. Accept. Capitalize.

During World War II car manufacturers re-tooled to make tanks. No one went broke. Throughout our history we've taken on challenges with the cooperation of business and government. The fossil fuel industry has known the reality of climate change for decades, but continued to fight any move to address the problem because they didn't want to change their business model. LBJ said, "Once you have them by the balls, their hearts and minds will follow." In this case, they've got us by the balls. But once they figure out how to fill their wallets, their hearts and minds will follow. Although they may not have much choice, as in December 2015, 195 countries ratified an agreement that would begin to limit greenhouse gas emissions, a crucial first step in dealing with a problem Republicans still won't publicly admit exists.

**THE LIE:
THE TAX SYSTEM IS
TOO COMPLICATED!
WE NEED A FLAT TAX!**

The truth: the so-called Flat Tax or Fair Tax is pure misdirection. Even though the argument sounds perfectly reasonable: just simplify the tax code by creating a single rate for everyone; say, 15%. Rand Paul aired commercials in June 2013, proclaiming that the IRS is taking away your freedoms, and advocated abolishing the agency, and instituting a fair tax. Sounds fair, right? And we're all about fair. Who doesn't like fair?

None of this is about being fair. Wealthy people and corporations just want to pay lower taxes and don't give a damn if you pay less, too. David Stockman, Ronald Reagan's budget director, admitted as much in 1981, stating, "the promise of tax cuts for everyone was always a Trojan Horse to bring down the top rate for the richest."

They also want less money coming into the government so they can defund every program they don't like. Republicans just want to, as Grover Norquist is all-too-often quoted, "starve the federal government until it's small enough to drown in a bathtub."

THE LIE:
THE DEATH TAX!

The inheritance tax. Also called a redistribution of wealth by many on the right. After all, as the argument goes, if someone makes billions, they should be allowed to pass it on. Why should someone's money be taxed twice? Once when they make it, and again when they die? It's not fair.

The truth: individuals get to pass on $5.43 million of their estate, tax free, to their heirs. Couples get to pass on $10.86 million. Guess how many Americans have a net worth over $10 million? 2 of every 1000 estates. That's 0.02% of the population. And the tax is not on the people who made the money. It's on the people who receive it. Like all income is taxed.

What's ironic is that the party decrying the Death Tax is also the party of hard work and self-reliance. They hate freeloaders and welfare queens. So, why are they so outraged over the prospect that there might be a few less over-privileged little shits in the world? They don't seem to be worried about the depletion of our natural resources, climate change, erratic weather patterns, rising sea levels, diminishing water supplies, polluted water, polluted air, rampant wild fires, gun violence, and fracking, but they're flipping out over the notion that our American way of life will disappear if we choke off our supply of Paris Hiltons.

THE LIE:
BARACK OBAMA
AND THE TERRIBLE, HORRIBLE,
NO GOOD VERY BAD IRAN NUKE DEAL!

Given the level of hysteria coming out of the GOP, you would have thought it was health care all over again, or an election year. "It's a terrible deal!" "Even worse than we thought!" And then there's Huckabee's comment that this deal will "take the Israelis and march them to the door of the ovens." Stay classy, Huck.

The truth: you don't negotiate with your friends. Ok, so maybe a Muslim country with nukes could destabilize the region and possibly usher in Armageddon. Sort of like if Pakistan had the bomb. Oh, wait. They do. Still, a nuclear Iran is not something anyone wants. Like when kids in the park wave around sharp sticks, no good is going to come of it. But, election year, anti-Democrat hysteria aside, there are some facts that just don't seem to make it into the conversation.

The U.S. didn't act unilaterally. Britain, France, Germany, China, and Russia were in on it. They can't all be feckless and naïve. And is Iran really that tough? Nothing against them, I'm sure they're a very attractive, very powerful country and could make life in the west miserable if they put their minds to it. They're certainly spoiling for a fight since the CIA helped topple their government in 1953 and stuck the Shah in power, which eventually lead to the Ayatollah Khomeini's return to power, and the taking of American hostages in 1979. Still, they're not Russia. And every U.S. president since the 1950s has struck a nuclear deal with the U.S.S.R/Russians, who have always had, and continue to have solid, world-destroying credibility.

In 1963, JFK signed the Nuclear Test Ban Treaty with the Soviets. In 1968, LBJ signed the Nuclear Non-Proliferation Treaty. In 1968, Nixon signed SALT 1 and an ABM treaty. In 1972, Ford negotiated the SALT 2 framework. In 1979, Carter signed SALT 2. In 1987, Reagan signed the Intermediate-Range Nuclear Forces Treaty, and established the foundation for START 1. In 1991, Bush 1 signed START 1. In 1993, Bush 1 signed START 2. In 1994, Clinton signed a deal with North Korea to end their pursuit of nuclear arms. In 2002, Bush 2 signed the Strategic Offensive Reduction Treaty.

A few other points: If it's about the billions Iran will get back, based on the lifting of sanctions, they've already been sponsoring terrorism with sanctions in place. Apparently, they found enough spare change in the couch cushions to engage in mischief. And if Iran were truly the scourge of the eastern world, we made their lives much easier by invading Iraq, getting rid of Saddam Hussein, and destabilizing that country.

And if, in 10 years, Iran somehow manages to fire off a nuke, the reprisals would be instantaneous. And overwhelming. We still have mutually assured destruction, although, in this case, the destruction wouldn't be mutual. They would be committing instant, national suicide.

History has proven one thing: you don't need millions of dollars or weapons of mass destruction to stage a terrorist attack. The Oklahoma City Federal Building bombing was pulled off with $5000 worth of chemicals, diesel fuel, fertilizer, and a Ryder truck. The 9/11 terrorists did it with a plan, box cutters, a perverted ideology and a death wish. Any group with enough financial resources could get their hands on some black market nuclear material, and whip up a dirty bomb. At the end of the day, terrorism isn't about flying planes into buildings, sending in suicide bombers, or shooting people in cities. It's about doing the unthinkable. Given that, anything is possible.

This deal will put off Iran's nuclear program for at least a decade. Who knows how different the world will be by then. The recent climate change agreement notwithstanding, we've dragged our feet on this problem for so long, in 10 years the surface temperature of the Earth could be 150 degrees and we'll all be living in underground climate-controlled bunkers. Why waste time worrying about Iran nuking us when we've been hell-bent on nuking ourselves?

THE LIE:
THE
HOLLYWOOD
LIBERAL ELITE

The truth: I've worked as a writer in Hollywood for over 25 years. And, yes, we have our share of liberals, also conservatives and libertarians. Frankly, in a town that rewards lying, greed, and unabashed self-interest, it's surprising there aren't more Republicans. I've met and worked with many conservatives, and even had a few enjoyable, civilized conversations, where there were some points of agreement, though many places where we clearly diverged. I've also been in situations where I've heard slyly muttered racist comments, sometimes intended as jokes, other times not. And other times, not quite so slyly muttered.

Even if Hollywood were predominantly liberal, conservatism is still alive and well. In May 2015, a group of conservative comedy writers was hard at work crafting anti-Obamacare YouTube videos, funded by the Heritage Foundation. And riding the wave of word vomit that has him leading the GOP field, Trump went to L.A. in July 2015, and met with a group of conservative actors and industry professionals calling themselves Friends of Abe. (I assume Abe refers to Lincoln, and not Vigoda. Look it up.)

According to an article on *The Daily Beast*, they're a "secretive group of Hollywood right-wingers, founded in 2005 as a GOP support group, and operating under the same PR rules as *Fight Club*." (I wonder if there's a secret Friends of Abe greeting. Maybe they wink, and then mime shooting themselves in the head.) I guess the reason for the secrecy is that they're afraid of being blackballed in liberal Hollywood should word of their political leanings leak out.

Oh, brave, noble industry professionals. Huddled in your cells, clutching your deep, dark conservative secret as close to your hearts as your dog-eared copies of *The Fountainhead*. Here's the thing: your political leanings are no secret, because you're not shy about expressing your opinions in public. And the media reports on it because many of you are among the richest, most successful people in Hollywood. Are you now or have you ever been a conservative? Bullfuck.

There is no liberal blacklist. Once upon a time, when the Red Scare was scary, there was a real anti-communist blacklist because the studio moguls didn't want to come off as commie sympathizers by hiring commie sympathizers, or actual commies, because they knew if the story got out, people wouldn't pay to see their commie movies. But these days, nobody cares. As the Friends of Abe well know, ultimately Hollywood doesn't discriminate based on politics. Or race. Or religion. Or going on a drunken tirade against Jews and calling a cop "sugar tits." Hollywood is about one thing and one thing only: money. They'd green-light a movie with Hitler and Satan if they thought it would have a $100 million opening weekend. (Note for screenplay: Hitler and Satan in a buddy comedy. Title: *Hellcats*. Or maybe *Fast and Fuhrious*. Maybe not.)

Conservatives have even had their own TV shows, some very successful, mostly the dramas, the comedies, not so much. Fox tried their version of news satire with *The ½ Hour News Hour*. It premiered in 2007, and was cancelled in 2007, after 13 episodes, for the simple reason that it was painfully unfunny. One thing Fox doesn't get is that in the world of mockery, they are the mockees, not the mockers. Their shows are already borderline self-parody.

Successful TV news satire has always leaned left. *That Was The Week That Was* on the BBC in the '60s. *Not Necessarily the News* ran on HBO for 8 years during the '80s. *Weekend Update* on *SNL* has been a staple of the show from the beginning. Jon Stewart retired after 16 brilliant seasons on *The Daily Show*. Trevor Noah has stepped into the role and demonstrated that he's got the wit to keep the franchise alive. Just as Larry Wilmore has done on *The Nightly Show*. John Oliver is crushing it on HBO, as is Samantha Bee on TBS. And Bill Maher has set the standard for humor and provocative political discourse on TV for 22 years, with shows on Comedy Central, ABC, and HBO. In the end, right wing comedy shows suck for the same reason right wing comics and Christian comics suck. It's amusing to make fun of assholes. It's not amusing to be them.

THE LIE:
THE LEFT/RIGHT EQUIVALENCY
OF FOX NEWS AND MSNBC

The truth: there is no equivalency. This is a grand macro lie put forth by Fox to legitimize their truth-bending by saying the other side does the same thing. So, let's put it to the test: I propose a debate, on a neutral network, with a neutral moderator, and a neutral fact checker; and no audience, so they can't paper the house with fake applause. On one side: Rachel Maddow, Lawrence O'Donnell, Chris Matthews, and Chris Hayes. On the other: Bill O'Reilly, Sean Hannity, Steve Doocy, and Megyn Kelly. No crib sheets. No notes written on palms, just an honest, televised debate. In your court, Fox.

THE LIE:
BARACK OBAMA IS THE
WORST PRESIDENT IN HISTORY!

The truth: At some point you have to wonder how Cheney, this deranged, sclerotic old fossil whose perfidy goes back to the Nixon years, can get up in the morning and look in a mirror, knowing that his administration was responsible for the single greatest national defense fuck-up of the 21st century, followed by the single greatest foreign policy screw-up of the 21st century, followed by the single greatest economic catastrophe since the Great Depression. Cheney worked

W. like some megalomaniacal Gepetto, pulling the strings on his little wooden boy to get him to invade Iraq. 4488 Americans dead, 32,223 wounded, 655,000 Iraqis dead. $1.7 trillion wasted. Lead to the creation of ISIS. Yeah, that's leadership.

For all the lies lobbed at this president over the last 7 years, let's check the score. He didn't take away our freedom, last I checked, I still had mine. No one killed grandma. Well, mine's been dead for 30 years, but I don't think Obama killed her. Then again, I can't confirm his whereabouts at the time. Despite Trump raising the birther nonsense again, no one's paying much attention. This shit scandal has fewer legs than Oscar Pistorius. Everyone's still got their guns. There have been no death panels. By every single metric, the economy is in recovery. There's been no war on the rich. No class warfare. Everyone's still free to practice their religion. Or not practice their religion. To the chagrin of the Christian right, it's not yet mandatory. We haven't gone socialist, communist, fascist, Marxist, or full-tilt monarchy, tyranny, or dictatorship. Whether we've gone oligarchy is probably up for debate in some circles. But, as of this writing, all three branches of government still have their appropriate powers and continue to slug it out.

So, in an effort to clear this up, let's compare the highlights of the Obama and Cheney/Bush administrations. (Let's not be disingenuous about who was really in charge. "I'm the decider" was a petulant child stomping his feet and insisting, "I am so the president! I am!")

THE CHENEY/BUSH RECORD

- ALLOWED 9/11 TO OCCUR, EVEN WITH PRIOR WARNING.
- STARTED THE IRAQ WAR BASED ON LIES, LEFT THE COUNTRY IN CHAOS, LEADING TO THE RISE OF ISIS.
- LEGALIZED TORTURE AT ABU GHRAIB AND GUANTANAMO.
- VOWED TO "SMOKE OUT" OSAMA BIN LADEN. DIDN'T.
- LET NEW ORLEANS DROWN AFTER KATRINA WITH A HACK POLITICAL APPOINTEE IN CHARGE OF FEMA.
- FIRED FEDERAL PROSECUTORS FOR REFUSING TO ENGAGE IN POLITICALLY MOTIVATED PROSECUTIONS.
- EXPOSED THE IDENTITY OF A CIA AGENT AS AN ACT OF POLITICAL RETRIBUTION.
- STONEWALLED ON CLIMATE CHANGE.
- TOOK OFFICE INHERITING A $127.3 BILLION SURPLUS, LEFT OFFICE WITH A $1.4 TRILLION DEFICIT.
- ENACTED ECONOMIC POLICIES THAT RESULTED IN THE LOSS OF 800,000 JOBS A MONTH.
- LEFT OFFICE WITH THE DOW AT 7900, GDP GROWTH AT 8.9%, AND UNEMPLOYMENT AT 7.2%.
- PRESIDED OVER A FINANCIAL MELTDOWN THAT NEARLY USHERED IN THE SECOND GREAT DEPRESSION.

THE OBAMA RECORD

- AGAINST REPUBLICAN DISASTER CRIES, USED TARP PROGRAM TO PULL ECONOMY OUT OF A POTENTIAL DEPRESSION.
- SAVED GM.
- NO 9/11-SCALE TERRORIST ATTACKS ON U.S. SOIL.
- OSAMA BIN LADEN KILLED.
- TROOPS WITHDRAWN FROM IRAQ.
- AGAINST A TIDAL WAVE OF REPUBLICAN OBJECTION PASSED THE AFFORDABLE CARE ACT, INSURING OVER 14 MILLION PEOPLE.
- AS OF 2016, THE DOW IS AROUND 17,000.
- UNEMPLOYMENT IS 5 %.
- CONSUMER CONFIDENCE UP 254%
- 14 MILLION JOBS CREATED OVER 71 STRAIGHT MONTHS OF PRIVATE SECTOR GROWTH.
- ESTABLISHED DIPLOMATIC RELATIONS WITH CUBA
- JOINED WORLD LEADERS IN RATIFYING 2015 PARIS CLIMATE CHANGE AGREEMENT.
- SIGNED DODD-FRANK WALL STREET REFORM AND CONSUMER PROTECTION ACT INTO LAW.

Even Fox can't spin these numbers. Not that it stops trying, and not that this president has been perfect. Perfection is an illusion. And the world's a mess. And there is no 11th commandment in the Democratic Party. We have no problem criticizing our own. Obama didn't shut down Guantanamo, although he's raising the issue again in early 2016. Troops are still in Afghanistan. We still have no definitive immigration policy. The NSA may have too much leeway when it comes to the invasion of our privacy, even with the 2015 revisions. The administration underestimated the threat posed by ISIS, which has expanded its repertoire from rampaging all over Iraq and Syria, to terrorist attacks in Beirut, Paris, and San Bernardino. And the Middle East is still a raging, internecine, religious/political clusterfuck that only seems to get more volatile and dangerous with each passing day.

But here's the ultimate hypocrisy: If you simply reversed these two records, and gave Obama's record to Bush, and Bush's to Obama, Republicans would be carving George Bush's face on the side of Mt. Rushmore. Bottom line, the left hated Bush because of what he did. And were complicit in quite a bit of it. Democrats, including Hillary, voted for the Iraq War. It was post-9/11. We were hysterical and wanted revenge. Like rebound sex after a break up, we just wanted to hate-fuck someone. We would have bombed Canada to get it out of our system.

The right hated Obama because of what he represented, personally, and politically. But of all the heinous crimes Obama and the Democrats have been accused of over the last seven years, the one they're actually guilty of is never mentioned: that of ceding the early narrative to the Republicans. Instead of coming out strong and touting their accomplishments they were reduced to forcing the president to hand over his birth certificate, in response to the inane accusations of a handful of lunatics and a Republican party that just smirked and let the clowns run amok. They relegated themselves to the role of defenders. The other crime was their naiveté in thinking the GOP was going to hold hands in some kind of bipartisan, legislative love fest. The president tried every method at his disposal: hands across the aisle, joint, working sessions. Even if they were photo ops devised for public shaming, they didn't work. You can't shame the shameless. And none of this won over a single Republican convert.

When the history of this period is written, it will show that Republicans acted despicably, dishonorably, and disrespectfully, obstructionist from start to finish, with no regard for how their conduct would affect the lives of Americans. Their cynical, single-minded efforts were about one thing: creating the meme that the election of the first African American president was a mistake.

To this day, I hear political pundits on TV describe the president as "polarizing." Please. From the day of his inauguration, right up to the present moment, President Obama has faced relentless, univocal opposition, and unprecedented disrespect. If a Democratic congressman blurted "you lie" at President Bush during a State Of The Union address, the Republican apoplexy machine would have gone into full metal freak-out. But this president handled it with class, intelligence, humor, and all the dignity one could ever want from a President of the United States. We may wallow around in the sty of petty politics, but history will give President Obama the praise he deserves. Frankly, if I were writing his post-term memoires, I'd title it "Fuck all y'all!"

With the 2016 elections in high gear, Republicans continue to spin the lie that this administration has been a failure, because it's their only road to reclaiming the presidency. And the same dumbass segment of the population believes it. Just look at who's leading the GOP field. But, at the end of the day, the problem isn't money, lies, propaganda, negative ads, dirty tricks, decentralized news, talking points, or trumped up investigations. The problem is that they work on us. And they work because we're uncritical, uneducated, and uninformed. A smarter electorate would be more skeptical of the lies. In fact, the incendiary tone and hyperbolic rhetoric in the message would instantly lead one to question the content.

And underlying our political gullibility is the fact that we don't think, we believe. We don't doubt. We follow. We don't question or challenge. We have faith. And at the root of much of this behavior is the undertow of stupidity in our lives that is our juvenile, superstition-based notion of religion.

Every step forward we've taken in this country has been with the shackles of religion holding us back. The religious right has stubbornly waged the culture wars, the attacks on Planned Parenthood, resisted the teaching of evolution, and relentlessly fear mongered about LGBT rights and gay marriage.

It's said that there are two things you don't talk to strangers about: politics and religion. I've already broken the first rule. Let's go knock off the second.

CHAPTER EIGHT

DUMBF**CK RELIGION

PART ONE

DECONSTRUCTION

"Religion easily has the best bullshit story of all time.
Think about it. Religion has convinced people
that there's an invisible man… living in the sky
who watches everything you do, every minute of every day. And
the invisible man has a list of ten specific things he
doesn't want you to do. And if you do any of these
things, he will send you to a special place of
burning and fire and smoke and torture
and anguish for you to live forever and suffer,
and burn, and scream until the end of time.
But he loves you. He loves you. He loves you, and
He needs money."
George Carlin

It's unlikely that any hard-core conservatives bought this book, let alone read this far. That would show an open-mindedness or strain of masochism they have yet to demonstrate. But if, by chance, some have, this will probably drive a stake through their hearts, while sending committed atheists running for the Valium. Because while our dialogue on politics and guns may be dumb, there's no conversation in American life as retarded as the one we have on religion.

We accept gravity, aerodynamics, photosynthesis, thermodynamics, relativity, quantum mechanics, sexual reproduction, rain, thunder, earthquakes, volcanoes, and tidal waves, all based on science. But when it comes to the origin and nature of life itself we take leave of our senses for a trip into the supernatural. We literally lose our minds.

Even though the Library of Congress houses 18 million books on 530 miles of bookshelves, including 54 million manuscripts, we're told that the truth of human existence can be found in literal interpretations of one of several centuries-old books, of dubious authorship, that are riddled with myth, prejudice and superstition. And no one questions it.

Despite advancements in medicine, we still light candles, engage in prayer circles, travel to Lourdes for magic healing waters, and get on our knees and pray to a statue in the hope that it can heal disease.

We've confused freedom of religion with the notion that any behavior or statement, no matter how idiotic or onerous, carries an inherent legitimacy, as long as it's grounded in someone's faith. For all our technical sophistication, when it comes to the subject of religion, we're so mired in ignorance and superstition we might as well be running around in animal skins, sacrificing goats, and throwing virgins into volcanoes. Chronologically this may be the 21st century, but intellectually it's the Dark Ages.

A recent Harris poll found that 74% of Americans believe in God. The study also revealed that 72% believe in miracles, 68% believe in Heaven, 65% believe that Jesus is God or the Son of God, 65% believe in the resurrection of Jesus Christ, 58% believe in the devil and hell, 57% believe in the virgin birth, 42% believe in ghosts, 36% believe in creationism and UFOs, 29% believe in astrology, 24% believe in reincarnation, and 26% believe in witches.

Of course, if you asked most Americans if they believed in Aphrodite, Apollo, Ares, Artemis, Asclepius, Astraea, Ate, Athena, Attis, Bia, Boreas, Caerus, Calliope, Calypso, Castor, Cerus, Ceto, Chaos, Charon, Chronos, Circe, Clio, Clotho, Crius, Cronus, Cybele, Demeter, Dinias, Dionysys, Eileithyia, Eirisone, Electra, Elpis, Enyo, Eos, Erato, Erebus, Eris, Eros, Eurus, Euturpe, Gaia, Giaucuc, Hades, Harmonia, Hebes, Helios, Hemera, Hephaestus, Hera, Heracles, Hermes, Hesperus, Hestia, Hygea, Hymenaios, Hypnos, Iris, Khione, Kotys, Lacheses, Mais, Mania, Melpomene, Merope, Metis, Momus, Morpheus, Nemesis, Nereus, Nike, Notus, Nyx, Oceanus, Pallas, Pan, Peitha, Persephone, Pheme, Phosphorus, Plutus, Polyhumnia, Pontus, Poseidon, Priapus, Pricus, Proteus, Rhea, Selene, Sterope, Styx, Tartarus, Taygete, Terpsichore, Thalia,

Thanatos, Themis, Thetis, Triton, Tyche, Typhon, Urania, Uranus, Zelus, Zephyrus, or Zeus they'd say of course not. Those are just the silly gods of primitive cultures. But suggest that belief in God might be just as silly and primitive, and they'll punch your face in for talking smack about their sky daddy.

The anthropomorphic God has been woven into the fabric of American life. "In God We Trust" is on the money, thus uniting the two things we worship – God and money – despite their contradictory impulses. Presidents swear to God they will faithfully execute the duties of their office. Witnesses in court, students reciting the Pledge, candidates during a campaign, no one gets by without invoking God. "God bless you and God bless the United States of America" is the standard closing line for any political address and, if omitted, leaves the candidate or office holder open to the double-edged attack of atheism and lack of patriotism.

Unfortunately, because religion is passed down via indoctrination, our thinking on the subject remains ridiculously primitive, riddled with superstition, and bizarre beliefs and practices ranging from naïve and ignorant, to deranged, delusional, and profoundly dumb. And while that might seem harsh, there are some ideas and behavior that don't rate nuance. They're just plain dumb. And it's a dumbness that spans all levels of society from the most Neanderthal, knuckle scraping high school dropout up to members of the media, Congress, and even a former president. Exactly what do I mean by dumb. These are actual news headlines:

*Kentucky High School Student Wouldn't Compete
in Race Because His Bib Number Was 666,
The Sign of the Devil*

*Kentucky Man Dies After Snakebite During
Pentecostal Church Service*

*Fox News Pastor: Jesus Wouldn't
Protect Undocumented Immigrants*

*Anti-gay Michigan Pastor Resigns
After Being Caught on Grindr*

*Executive Vice President of the Family
Research Council says Jesus Will
Return to Earth with an AR-15 Rifle*

*Liberty University President says, "If more people
had concealed guns, we could end those Muslims"*

*Minnesota Archbishop Claims Satan is Behind
Gay marriage, Condoms and Porn*

*Pat Robertson Says 2015 Stock Market
Crash is God's Punishment for Planned Parenthood*

Fight Over School Prayer Turns Ugly

Exorcism Performed in Texas Park

Conservative Bible Project Cuts Out Liberal Passages

*Christian Radio Host: "God Let Kids Die in Sandy Hook
Massacre as Punishment For the Blood of the Unborn"*

*Tennessee County Lawmakers Will Vote to Ask God to
Spare His Wrath over Marriage Equality*

*Parents Arrested After 19-Year-Old
Dies in Church "Counseling Session"*

*Christian Radio Host: "Ebola Could End
Atheism, Homosexuality, Sexual Promiscuity,
Pornography, and Abortion"*

Even on the rare occasion when a civilized discussion of religion occurs, it's usually rooted in a single question: do you believe in God? If the answer is "no," the typically petulant comeback is: "Then what do you believe?" Americans get offended when anyone questions their beliefs without stopping to wonder why it's necessary for a person to have beliefs, over and above actual knowledge and experience.

Our conversation on religion is based on an unfortunate paradigm that's been passed down through the millennia like a game of telephone, in which one is a believer, atheist, or agnostic. Believers cling to their beliefs, and you challenge them at your own risk. To atheists, religion is just a nonsensical collection of ghost stories and fairy tales for people who don't have the wherewithal to deal with life based on reason and reality. As for agnostics, they're just intellectual eunuchs who think they're demonstrating great equanimity by throwing their hands in the air, proclaiming, "maybe there's a God, maybe there's isn't. It's all too mysterious for we humans to know." These stale categories have framed our discussion about religion on TV, in classrooms, even in the media. People yell, scream, rant and rave about religion, yet have no idea what it really is, what purpose it's supposed to serve, or why it even exists in the first place.

Religion is no different from any other area of study man has devised to examine the phenomenon of life; history, science, psychology, sociology, anthropology. Each discipline micro-focuses on a specific aspect of life, both to examine that one area and, by extension, understand how it functions as part of the whole. To say we can think, analyze, or discuss every single aspect of our lives, holding ideas up to the light of reality, but that this same standard can't apply to religion is nonsense. It's not that religion is so trivial that it's unimportant. It's that it's too important to be trivialized.

In 2010 I wrote a book – *Deconstructing God – A Heretic's Case for Religion.* (In the interest of full disclosure, I've excerpted certain passages in this book. My words, I can use them where I want.) At the time my hope was that it would open up a dialogue leading to an understanding of the core experience underlying each religious tradition, and usher in a period of mutual respect and peace on Earth from now until the end of time. My goals might have been a tad presumptuous. So, I'll try again.

In 1517 Martin Luther nailed his 95 Theses to the door of the All Saints Church, ushering in the Reformation. Maybe it's time for a second reformation, only this time, instead of railing against corruption and the selling of indulgences, we can rail against superstition and stupidity, with the goal of arriving at a more subtle and sophisticated understanding of the subject. Toward that end, I offer a primer: 50 Truths About Religion.

<u>50 TRUTHS ABOUT RELIGION</u>

ONE

There is no God. Not in the beginning. Not now. Not ever. It's ok. Take a deep breath and let it sink in. It's not a matter of opinion. There are no two sides to the argument. There simply is no God. No magical, sky daddy creator of the universe who lives in a place called Heaven. Despite the fact that the Old Testament God is the foundation of the Judeo/Christian/Islamic traditions, He doesn't exist. Never has. Never will. How do we know there's no God, beyond the simple fact that the notion of a creator of the universe is childish and silly?

TWO

Evidence: God has never revealed Himself in any verifiable way, which He can't, because He doesn't exist. Somehow, in the case of *Religion v. Atheists*, the basic structure of the American legal system has been inverted, so that instead of placing the burden of proof on the prosecution -- the side making the allegation – the burden of disproof has been placed on the defense, as if the hypothesis has been established and remains in place until it can be successfully rejected.

THREE

Reason vs. belief. Any word, system, or theory should be evaluated solely on the basis of whether it accurately describes the world. The goal is to explain what is the case, not what people wish were the case, think is the case, or believe with all their heart is the case. Belief in the existence of a proposition does not establish its validity.

FOUR

Idol worship. Man made a great intellectual leap from polytheism to monotheism, from the idea of many Gods to just the one. But worshipping the anthropomorphic God is essentially practicing virtual idolatry -- monotheism, with a polytheistic mindset. According to the Old Testament, Moses received the Ten Commandments on Mt. Sinai but smashed them on the ground when he saw his people dancing around a golden calf. Most religious people think they're on the mountain with Moses, when, in fact, they're on the ground dancing around a statue, or in this case, an invisible idol.

FIVE

Reality. Reality 3500 years ago is the same as reality today. Gravity then is gravity now. Therefore, since we don't have angels, parting seas, or virgin mommies, and no one comes back from the dead or heals lepers by touch, it becomes a very simple equation: if it can't happen now, it couldn't have happened then. Religion exists in reality, not outside of it.

SIX

Oversimplification. The origin of the universe must be as complex as the universe itself. It's the goal of science to observe phenomena and develop theories, many of which will change over time to accommodate new data. The notion that there is some great cosmic intelligence behind it all is a ridiculous oversimplification. When the science behind natural phenomena didn't exist, it's understandable that people would reach for simpler explanations. But here in the 21st century, it's absurd. To understand how the world came to be, look to the God Particle, not God.

SEVEN

Paternalistic language and psychological need. People afraid of facing the prospect of being alone in their lives, or in the universe, cling to the security of childhood by positing a Big Daddy in control. Scientific immaturity meets emotional insecurity. And it's reflected in religious language.

God is lord, king, our father. And we're His children. God is omniscient. Omnipotent. He loves us, watches over us, and never leaves. Does it really take a giant mental leap to see the need being filled? No wonder people get so emotional when the existence of God is questioned. The movement from childhood to adulthood necessitates leaving home and living without daddy's guidance. Who's ready to go it alone? Who wouldn't like the idea of daddy always being there? It provides a feeling of warmth and comfort, along with the security of being unconditionally loved. The uneasiness or hostility exhibited by some when they're told there's no God is an outward manifestation of their inner existential anxiety.

They also think there's a man in the sky who's omniscient and omnipotent enough to create an entire universe, and yet who is simultaneously so thin-skinned as to get wrathful and vindictive when anyone doubts His existence. This actually reveals more about us than it does about the world. If we define our God as angry and wrathful it's because we're angry and wrathful and we're trying to justify these attitudes by claiming they reflect objective reality.

EIGHT

Arrogance. We think we've been lovingly placed on this tiny spec of space dust by a benevolent father figure whose got a super special plan for each one of our lives, and afterlives. We also think He loves one particular group more than any other. Of course, which group that is depends on whether you're talking to Jews, Christians, or Muslims.

Even if you believe there is a God who created everything, do you really think He looked out on the entire universe, then focused on this tiny planet, then further zoomed in on a particular group of people and thought, "I like these people more than all those other people I created." And then picked out a plot of land and said, "I want them, and only them, to live there." God, not just as loving father, but as real estate agent.

NINE

Alternate religious ideas. 65% of religious people do not base their practice on the Old Testament God. The existence or non-existence of the personal God has been the main difference between the eastern and western traditions, but the argument has been posed as if they represent two equally legitimate points of view. They don't.

TEN

Religion has absolutely nothing to do with the origins of the physical universe. Creationism, or its barely literate cousin, Intelligent Design, are pathetic attempts to tart up superstition as science and legitimize myth as fact, based on the false premise that if the Genesis thread is pulled, the entirety of religion unravels. So, instead of using reason to separate myth from science, and history from allegory, reason was sent on a fool's errand to prove the necessity of a creator. Clinging to Genesis as the *sine qua non* of religion is just as invalid as rejecting the totality of religion because of it. It's not a matter of faith vs. reason. It's a matter of reason vs. lack of reason.

Science examines the origin and nature of the physical universe. When properly understood and practiced, religion explores a deeper, more profound experience of human life. They have absolutely nothing to do with one another.

ELEVEN

So, if there's no God, then why are we here? We're here because we're here. The world came into existence and evolved over billions of years. If conditions hadn't been right for life to occur, we simply wouldn't exist. Our world is a reflection of who we are and how we evolved. The mistake is finding ourselves alive on Earth and assuming we were meant to be here, instead of merely appreciating the fact that we are. We can appreciate our reality without assuming our necessity.

TWELVE

What about beauty? Doesn't the beauty in nature necessitate intention? How could sunsets be an accident? Because they are. Sunsets exist. Man perceives them because he has eyes and finds them appealing. He then creates a word like "beauty" to communicate that feeling. If, instead of a stunning light show, the end of the day was marked by people getting struck by lightning, we wouldn't be waxing quite so poetic about sunset. It would be more like "Oh, fuck! It's sunset!"

THIRTEEN

What about morality and codes of behavior? Don't they need to be handed down from some higher power? No. In *The Brothers Karamazov*, Dostoevsky wrote: "If there is no God, then everything is permitted." But that's based on the false notion that we are children who require rules from some stern parent. Concepts of ethics and morality are man-made. Absolute morality is like blind justice. Not something that exists, as such, but something man created as an ideal to shoot for -- a guiding principle.

The assumption that ethical behavior involves commandments from some higher power has left us with a group of so-called religious leaders who don't understand the difference between morality and moralizing. Morality is about teaching you how to live with your neighbor. Moralizing is about trying to tell your neighbor how to live.

FOURTEEN

What about the human body; the mechanics of the heart, the precision of the eye? Those sophisticated mechanisms couldn't possibly have come into existence by accident. Yes, they could. And they did. If we didn't have eyes, our world would have evolved to accommodate our blindness. If we didn't have ears, there'd be no verbal communication. Music might just be percussion, like in that Broadway show where they stomp around whacking garbage cans.

We're here because we evolved into creatures who were able to survive. And we continually adapt our world to our abilities and limitations. As a rebuttal to every "human eye" argument, I suggest you check out the *2015 Physicians' Desk Reference, 69th Edition;* 2500 pages detailing every nasty disease and affliction known to man.

And if that doesn't put you off the perfection of the divinely created human body, think about this: shit. That's right. Shit. Because when it came to the elimination of food waste, any intelligence that could craft an entire universe could have come up with something better. He could have made us differently, eliminating the byproduct entirely. He could have had us sweat it out, sneeze it out, or pop it out of our mouths like breath mints, or out our butts in perfumed sachets that not only delighted the senses but also gave an aromatic mist to the air. We could have literally been a species whose shit didn't stink.

So, if you believe that God created man, then the following conversation, dramatized for entertainment purposes, would have had to occur.

"SHIT"
A SHORT PLAY

EXT. HEAVEN – SEVENTH DAY

AFTER CREATING THE UNIVERSE AND EVERYTHING IN IT, GOD IS ABOUT TO REST, WHEN THERE'S A KNOCK AT THE GATES. IT'S AN ANGEL.

GOD: What?! I'm resting!
ANGEL: There's a problem.
GOD: What problem? I created a perfect universe. In 6 days, bitches! 6 days! So, piss off!
ANGEL: Ok, if that's the way you want it.
GOD: You know I hate that passive/aggressive crap. What's the problem?
ANGEL: It's people. Well, and animals, but the people are the ones doing all the bitching.
GOD: I knew they'd be annoying as soon as I gave them speech. Maybe I'll just kill 'em off.

THE ANGEL SHRUGS AND STARTS TO WALK AWAY.

GOD: Where are you going?
ANGEL: You just said…
GOD: I was venting, you idiot! What's the people problem?
ANGEL: They're dying.
GOD: I know they're dying. I made 'em that way so they wouldn't get uppity and forget who's in charge.
ANGEL: No, I meant they're dying, like quickly. It's the food.
GOD: Bullshit. The food's perfect. Plants. Vegetables. Grains. Water. If they're bored, tell 'em they can eat each other.
ANGEL: They already are. Thing is, it's giving off waste and it's poisoning them.
GOD: Christ, it's like I have to think of everything! (BEAT. HE THINKS, THEN GRABS A STAFF AND HANDS IT TO THE ANGEL.) Here. Poke a hole in the front, hole in the back, bad stuff comes out. Problem solved. Now, beat it.

THE ANGEL EXITS.

EXT. HEAVEN – A HALF HOUR LATER

GOD IS RESTING. THERE'S ANOTHER KNOCK ON THE DOOR.

GOD: What now?! Can't a brother get a nap?!
ANGEL: There's another problem.
GOD: For an angel, you're really pissing me off. Ask Lucifer how that worked out. (BEAT) Did you poke the holes?
ANGEL: Yes.

GOD: Did the stuff come out?
ANGEL: Yes.
GOD: Are they still dying?
ANGEL: No.
GOD: So, it works. Done, done, and done.
ANGEL: Yes, it works, but –
GOD: But what?! What?! What's the problem now?!
ANGEL: It stinks.
GOD: Stinks? What stinks?
ANGEL: The stuff that comes out.
GOD: What do you mean it stinks? Stinks like what?
ANGEL: Well… like shit.
GOD: Oh… (HE THINKS FOR A MOMENT.) You know what, I gave 'em life, food, sex, laughter, and baseball. They're just gonna have to fuckin' deal.

THE ANGEL SHRUGS AND EXITS. GOD TURNS OVER AND TAKES A WELL-DESERVED REST.

THE END

FIFTEEN

Religion has nothing to do with belief in God, creation myths, miracles, angels, saints, magic waters, messiahs, prophets, or divinely mandated codes of behavior via some incendiary shrub. Religious language is metaphorical and poetic. Genesis isn't history or science. It's poetry. The man who wrote, "the hand of God moved across the face of the waters" wasn't writing about a real hand, or a real God. He was trying to convey an experience of the pristine beauty of nature using poetic imagery.

Think of T.S. Eliot's poem: *The Wasteland*. The first line is: "April is the cruellest month." If you were trying to understand the writer's intent, would you Google "disasters in April"? Or might you think he was trying to evoke an emotion by juxtaposing a time of the season that's about hope with the pain we endure in our lives.

The Garden of Eden is not a place. It's a metaphor. We're not born in sin. We're not born in shame. We're just born. If the fall from grace has any meaning, it has to do with losing our sense of wonder and identity with all things as we grow conscious of our individuality. Also, and this is just for fun, Google Adam and Eve and check out the images. Note that in most, if not all of the depictions, Adam and Eve have navels. Given the Garden of Eden story, how'd that happen? Seems a few Renaissance artists didn't get the memo.

SIXTEEN

But isn't religion about faith? No. Sure, given the chaos of life, both natural and man-made, it's comforting to believe there's some benign intentionality behind it all, and that things always turn out for the best. Thinking this way can give people strength to persevere in hard times. Yet, experientially, there's little difference between saying "I have faith in God," and "I believe life is good." Either can give one hope, and the strength to deal with adversity.

But, ultimately, as far as our lives are concerned, we live and we die in a universe that just doesn't care. In fact, given life's inevitable conclusion, pessimism should be the more logical philosophical stance. It just doesn't lead to much joy. And if you spend your life obsessing over the fact that one day you're doing to die, two things will happen: One, you'll waste precious time fretting over the fact that some disease will eventually kill you; and two, one day you'll be right. When facing reality, hope is a defiant, existential choice. There's just no need for God to get there.

SEVENTEEN

What about worship? Isn't religion about worshipping the divine? No. *Baruch atah adonai elohaynu melech haolam* is the cornerstone of many Jewish prayers. During my adolescence I stood in temple mindlessly repeating it. Then, as an adult, I actually listened to the words: "Blessed art thou o lord our God, King of the Universe." What? As vast as it as, the universe has some sovereign ruling over it? And I'm supposed to go into a special building once a week and get down on my knees like a subject in King Arthur's court and prostrate myself before the universal King? Screw that. The only 2000-year-old man I worship is Mel Brooks.

And, as an interesting sidebar, when you realize there's no God, or devil, not only does belief become silly, but movies like *The Exorcist* and *The Omen* instantly turn into comedies. Well made, yet fundamentally comical. You don't even need to get high to watch them that way. Linda Blair levitating over the bed, face scratched up, head spinning around and howling like a demon while Max von Sydow flings holy water at her, bellowing, *"THE POWER OF CHRIST COMPELS YOU!!"* Hilarious.

EIGHTEEN

What about the afterlife? Steven Hawking referred to the afterlife as a fairy tale for people afraid of the dark. Much like the personal God, this notion is so ingrained in our thinking that, in trying to debunk it, one has to disprove the existence of something that can't be proven to exist. And the agnostic argument is even more irritating. "Maybe there's an afterlife. Maybe there isn't. We just can't know." These people you just want to smack in the head and spirit them directly to the afterlife they think may exist.

Like it or not, your personality is a phenomenon that comes into existence after you're born, and ceases to exist when you die, like a wave rolling in off the ocean, or wind rustling through the trees. Of course, no one likes to hear this. It's normal to be attached to the lives we've made. We put all this effort into family, friends, job, and home, and suddenly it's like we're mugged and it's all taken away. The discomfort people exhibit when it's suggested that death is the end is a reflection of their fear of non-existence. After all, who wouldn't want to believe that we all go on to some magical place in the sky? But it's wish fulfillment. Not fact. But the afterlife fairy tale just won't go away. It's not only infected the conversation about religion, but the entire culture.

NINETEEN

In 2003, a three-year-old preacher's son, Colton Burpo, (real name) had a near-death experience, but survived. Upon returning to consciousness he not only claimed he met his great-grandpa, but that he saw Jesus riding a rainbow-colored horse and later sat on his lap while Jesus sang to him.

Now, did the adult world realize that these were just the adorably precocious statements of a child who cheated death, using the language and imagery a preacher's son would have at his disposal? No. Instead, the father wrote a book: *Heaven is for Real: A Little Boy's Astounding Trip to Heaven and Back.*

And did the adult world realize that this book was probably just an expression of the joy his parents felt at having their son back with them? No. The book was published, and within three weeks of its November 2010 release debuted at number three on *The New York Times* Best Seller List, where it spent 206 weeks. It eventually sold 10 million copies. Once upon a time, children's literature referred to books written for children, not by them.

And did that end this little fairy tale? No. In May 2011, Sony bought the film rights and made it into a movie called *Heaven is For Real,* starring Greg Kinnear. It was released in 2014. The family even made an appearance on *The Today Show* to promote the release. The film grossed $91 million.

Coincidentally, in 2004, a six-year-old spent two months in a coma following a car accident. He was a quadriplegic, and not expected to survive. But when he came out of his coma he also told a tale of meeting Jesus. He, too, wrote a book with his father: *The Boy Who Came Back From Heaven: A Remarkable Account of Miracles, Angels, and Life Beyond This World.* It was also made into a movie. Then in early 2015, the kid released a statement confessing that he made the whole thing up just to get attention. The boy's name is Alex Malarkey. Malarkey, as in slang for bullshit.

TWENTY

What about reincarnation? There have been about 108 billion people alive on Earth. How could every one of those individual lives have some kind of cosmic, eternal staying power? What part of YOU do you think transcends death and inhabits a new body? If that were true of everyone who ever lived, then they've all been reincarnated into YOU. Which would mean that YOU are not really YOU. And if that were the case, given all the personalities in our heads, we'd all be raging schizophrenics, which would probably make daily life more frenetic, and drug companies ecstatic.

The YOU you know didn't exist before you were named, and raised in a particular environment. YOU are the result of the circumstances of your life. So, why do you think YOU would exist beyond your death? Imagine that right after you were born, a deranged person slipped into the hospital, snatched you out of your bassinette, raced to the airport, and flew you halfway around the world to be adopted by some childless couple and raised in a completely different culture, under a completely different name. Where would the YOU you know be? YOU wouldn't exist. So how could YOU be eternal?

Religion has nothing whatsoever to do with anything that happens after death, whether based on one's piety, frequency of churchgoing, baptism, or confession. Nothing happens after death. There's no judgment day. No pearly gates or day of reckoning that determines your post-death disposition. There's no moral pecking order to the universe, karmic or otherwise, nor any hierarchy of states of being in which one's behavior determines one's level of reincarnation, like getting some cosmic job promotion. All this talk about an afterlife isn't rational. It's emotional. So, let it go and relax. It's just death; it's not like it's the end of the world.

TWENTY-ONE

What about Heaven and Hell? Heaven and hell are metaphors. God and the devil are just the outward manifestations of our inner psychological impulses. There is no system of justice built into the world. No karmic payback. No reward or punishment for one's behavior. That is a misinterpretation of the idea of Karma, which differs in the Hindu and Buddhist traditions, but is defined as "action" and is meant to convey the idea that our lives are not predetermined by birth. We have the freedom to act.

Terms like rebirth, eternal life, or the Kingdom of Heaven, are not temporal, or geographical. They're psychological. Jesus' rebirth was about psychological transformation, not physical transportation. As it says in the Thomas Gospel: "The kingdom of heaven is within you."

TWENTY-TWO

We are the unwitting victims of a misunderstanding of religion, mired in centuries-old prejudices and ignorance. Instead of putting us more in touch with our true nature, religion, as it's understood and practiced in our culture, has disconnected us from who and what we really are. From the moralizing of the Christian right to the cruelty and misogyny of Sharia Law, the result is a perverted understanding of our basic, biological nature, particularly when it comes to our urge to procreate. You could call it Religion's Unholy Trinity: Sex, Homosexuality, and Abortion.

SEX

How did it happen that we've become so disconnected from such an essential part of who and what we are? Somehow, we've become alienated from the aspects of life that are most natural to us; namely: sex, bodily functions, bodily fluids, and death. It's as if western civilization is in rebellion against its own nature, and religion is in the forefront of the fight.

Sex is the original pleasure. Not the original sin. Sex isn't inherently salacious or sordid. It just is. Life is horny. The joy of sex is the delicious, delirious experience of DNA, giddy at the prospect of self-replication. Biologically, we're no different from any other creature on the planet. You see two dogs humping on the front lawn, or a couple of whales rolling around in the ocean, that's us. We just don't like to admit it. One could also make the case that it's something we do to feel less isolated in the universe. Trapped in our bodies and subjective experience, we literally connect with another human being.

Sex feels good. If sex were painful, there'd be 8 people on Earth, and procreation would involve some sort of mandatory duty, like military service in Israel. People would literally have to be drafted into the Fucking Army, where they'd be woken up at 4 am by a drill sergeant banging two garbage can covers together, and ordering soldiers to slide over in their bunks to let naked female cadets slip in next to them.

Sex didn't arrive with a playbook. Sexual taboos are man's invention. Sexual repression and misogyny are the result of a paternalistic society with a fundamental disconnect from its own basic nature. From angry, gynophobic mullahs hell-bent on covering women up to their eyeballs, to the denizens of Vatican City, who look and dress like a bunch of drag queens, some truly perverted individuals have been allowed to make the sex rules for everyone else.

Marriage is man made, not something instituted by God, though His name serves as one hell of a celebrity endorsement, while adding gravitas to the whole affair. Marriage has more to do with property, family structure, and maintaining social stability. And monogamy is its cornerstone. Besides, if everyone were having sex with everyone else, we'd never get any work done. And with the resulting jealousy and crimes of passion, we'd end up killing each other even more than we already do.

Societal mores and customs regarding sex vary from culture to culture. At our most enlightened, we try to teach children about sex while encouraging them to act responsibly so they don't end up pregnant too young. Though in societies where life expectancy is shorter, who's to say that having kids when the body is ready is unnatural? Kids grow up. Hormones kick in. You can't beat down a boner with a Bible. You have to teach a kid what to do with it, and what not to do. Telling teenagers to hold off on sex while trying to shame or frighten them out of masturbation is cruel and unusual punishment. Now that is hell.

We need to remove the curse put on sex by religion, and raise children in an environment where they're not scared out of their minds about things occurring naturally in their bodies. That doesn't mean letting kids run wild. It means teaching them the truth. When you demonize a child's natural feelings, you are building a person who is at war with him or herself. Hence the schizophrenic nature of our attitudes toward sex in western culture where we rail against it on Sunday from the pulpit, and celebrate it the other 6 days of the week.

The true purpose of religion is to put people more in touch with who they are. Original sin is not a prohibition against pre-marital orgasm. The fall from grace is a metaphor for man becoming disconnected from his essential self. It is psychological -- not sexual.

HOMOSEXUALITY

Even if you believe that a divine, omnipotent, omniscient God created the heavens and Earth, day and night, water, land, trees, plants, the stars, all living creatures on land, sea, and air, and blessed them all, saying, "be fruitful and multiply," do you really think that after that once-in-a-lifetime, monumental accomplishment, He looked at it all, pronounced it good, then was about to lie down and rest on the seventh day when He suddenly sprang up, smacked this head, and said, "Oh, wait! One more thing: No tushie sex!" If your answer is yes, then you're a fucking idiot.

Once again, religion has found a way to ignore the facts and stake a claim in the land of ignorance, fear, prejudice and superstition. So, let's break this down, real simple. Try to follow along. It doesn't matter that it's written in *Leviticus* that "lying with a man as with a woman is an abomination" and that "they shall surely be put to death," because those words were written by men, over 3500 years ago, and we've learned a few things since then.

Calling homosexuality a "lifestyle choice" is dumb. There's no other word for it. It's dumb. Homosexuality exists. It has always existed in a certain percentage of the population. Statistics vary, but for argument's sake, let's call it 5%, which is within the range of most studies. The exact number doesn't matter. What matters is that it's a real human phenomenon.

There are about 7 billion people on the planet, which would mean that, at this moment, there are roughly 350 million gay people all over the world. Do you really think that those 350 million people, from every culture, and from every kind of family background, spontaneously made the same lifestyle choice? Do you really think all those men thought, "Hmm...I love women, the way they smell. Taste. Feel. But damn if those gay guys don't dress nice. And they seem to have such a delightfully irreverent sense of humor. So I think I'll risk being ostracized by friends and family, ridiculed, beaten or murdered, sacrifice marriage and family, invite social ridicule, be treated like a second-class citizen, and have to fight for my basic civil rights by being gay." Similarly, do you really think all those women mused, "Well, I am attracted to men. And would love to get married one day and have children, but, damn if the siren song of the lesbian biker gang isn't way too strong."

Often in this discussion, the phrase "it's not normal" creeps in. But, once again, terms have to be defined. Homosexuality is not the norm, in the sense that it's not the experience of 95% of the population. But it is normal in the sense that it occurs naturally and spontaneously in human beings. Look at the language people use about coming out. It's language that describes feelings that have been kept hidden, by people denying who they really are. Trying to make the case that this is a lifestyle choice is the language of religious prigs working out their fears and, given the percentages, their self-loathing and internal conflicts.

Religion just has to let this one go already and stop promoting fear and hatred. Something they're not supposed to do in the first place. Homosexuality is what some people feel naturally when they've been served a different hormonal cocktail. It's about consenting adults, and what consenting adults consent to do in their consenting adulthood, should be their own consenting adult business. Frankly, if religion were to voice an opinion, it ought to be on the side of tolerance, something many religious types don't seem to get.

It may have taken centuries to overturn discriminatory laws, but it will take even longer to expunge ignorance and stupidity from the human heart. Not that many years ago women couldn't vote, black people weren't people, and interracial marriage was outlawed. Eventually we come around, as narrow minds die out, and society sheds ancient prejudices and superstitions. Unfortunately, people suffer along the way.

Even though the Supreme Court has legalized gay marriage, the Christian right is hardly going down without a fight. Twenty-one states have introduced so-called Religious Freedom bills, all as a smokescreen to justify discrimination by hiding behind the tattered robes of religion. The Reverend Pat Robertson reacted to Maine's becoming the 5th U.S. state to allow gay marriage by saying that it would be "the legalization of polygamy, bestiality, child molestation, and pedophilia." Maybe Pat should consider the possibility that Jesus was gay. After all, he was an unmarried guy in his 30s who wore robes, and traveled around with 12 male friends. And when he thought he was going to die, did he have one last sexual fling? No. He threw a dinner party for his guy friends and got kissed by one of them in a garden.

ABORTION

Despite the labels each camp has adopted: Right to Life, on the one hand, and Right to Choose on the other, no one in their right mind is pro-abortion. No 16-year-old thinks: "Damn, I'm pregnant and unmarried, and if I don't get on a reality show, my parents are going to kill me. But on the upside, at least I get to have an abortion!" The debate seems to hinge on the single question of when life begins and this is an area where those on the choice side have occasionally turned a deaf ear to an emotional reality.

The moment life begins is not something that can be discovered because "begins" is a man-made concept. We know how it happens. But who can point to the moment "it" starts and definitively pronounce a fertilized egg a person? Still, anyone who has had a child and looked at that first ultrasound of the little pea inside with the beating heart can't escape the feeling of awe that a new life has begun, self-aware or not. Feeling pain or not. Developed central nervous system or not. Something new has occurred. And those feelings should not be discounted. It makes it easier to understand the passion and outrage of the anti-abortion side and it's neither fair nor accurate to trivialize those emotions. There was a casual attitude to abortion in the '60s and '70s that did a disservice to the reality.

Yet, science has given us the option of abortion. Obviously, the goal of any sane society should be to reduce the number of abortions. But that goal can only be achieved through sex education. You can't put a lid on hormones. They're going to come out. Parents and schools need to educate kids about things that will happen to their bodies. To ignore the subject as if it doesn't exist, to force abstinence, or to try to shame teenagers out of their natural feelings gives rise to confusion, more teenage pregnancies, and more abortions. In this case, religion is the cause of its own worst nightmare.

If sex education was more honest, and modes of contraception more easily obtainable, the need for abortions would decrease. Though the heat of the moment will always be there and pregnancy will occasionally be the result. The solution is in the middle. Religious moralists just have to accept that sex is not evil, nor only sanctioned for marriage or procreation. Once teenage hormones start raging they don't stop. It's the life force in action and you can't outlaw it, legislate against it, or pretend it doesn't exist.

As for the morality involved, it's stated as an absolute: Abortion is murder. It's carried to the extreme when the bombing of an abortion clinic, murders at Planned Parenthood, or the shooting of an abortion doctor, in church no less, is perverted into a Christian thing to do. And yet those who take that stance often seem to be the same people supporting our troops, or calling for capital punishment. You can't take the moral high ground and outlaw abortion as murder if you simultaneously sanction murder, or war, however holy and noble in intent. Because if abortion is murder, then war and execution are murder, which leaves one, at least on the theoretical level, open to the same charge of moral relativism and situational ethics traditionally hurled at the secular left by the extreme right.

Also, as something for the pro-war crowd to ponder: with all the bombs dropped in all our noble wars, resulting in the occasional collateral damage -- the military euphemism for civilians being killed -- do you think some of those civilians might have been women? And do you think some of those women might have been pregnant? Perhaps some 2016 GOP presidential candidates need to sort out how their raging desire to carpet bomb the shit out of ISIS and kill all their families squares with their moral opposition to abortion.

Both sides want it both ways, which is never a recipe for solving a problem or arriving at some manageable middle ground. Defunding Planned Parenthood, closing abortion clinics, and shaming women out of having abortions serve no beneficial purpose. It's one thing to make a young woman aware of the option to carry a child to term and put it up for adoption. It's another to frighten an already frightened teenager to coerce her into the only option one finds morally acceptable.

TWENTY-THREE

What about miracles? There are no miracles. Sometimes the unexpected happens. A plane crashes killing hundreds of people, but one person survives. Suddenly the survivor is thanking God for the appeal, as opposed to cursing Him out for killing his fellow passengers and scaring the crap out of him. It never seems to occur to the survivor that maybe God didn't spare his life. Maybe God just missed. Or maybe the survivor just got lucky.

TWENTY-FOUR

What about prayer? Prayer is an internal mechanism for opening the heart. Not a form of two-way communication or a vehicle for petitioning some higher power for a bike at Christmas, or a cure for Grandma's cancer. Look at it rationally: Take 100 terminally ill patients. Then take 100 prayer circles around them, days and weeks of praying non-stop. Then 99 of those patients die anyway. But one survives. Do we ever hear the stories of all the failed prayer attempts? No. The only story that appears in the media is the one about the miracle survivor, the healing power of prayer, and the angels who were looking over them. But what about all the patients who just died? Were the angels too busy, or just apathetic?

It's human to want to reach out for help when you're feeling hopeless. It's comforting to think there's someone to whom you can pray, who's got the power to save you. But travelling to Lourdes in the hope of a cure for some disease is magical thinking, a genuine Hail Mary. There's no such thing as magic water, or holy water. There's just water.

TWENTY-FIVE

What about those who claim to speak for God? Villains, thieves, and con artists. God is not an entity and, therefore, cannot speak to pastors or endorse political candidates. When a preacher or politician claims their efforts are part of God's plan, they should have a net thrown over them. Anyone who claims to speak for God is either crazy, or lying for power or money. Or both. Think about it: if you were omnipotent and omniscient enough to create an entire universe, would you waste your time talking to a schmuck like Pat Robertson?

TWENTY-SIX

What about megachurches? Only in American could we conflate the two things we worship: God and money. In March 2014, Joel Osteen reported that $600,000 was robbed from the safe at his ministry. It was the proceeds from two days' take. Six hundred grand in two days; I thought Jesus threw the moneychangers <u>out</u> of the temple.

Despite the phrase: "it's easier for a camel to pass through the eye of a needle than for a rich man to get into heaven," we still hold on to the so-called prosperity gospel, based on the idea that the magic man in the sky wants you to be rich.

It's gotten so absurd that in early 2015, an Atlanta area pastor, ironically named Creflo Dollar, produced a video asking people for $300 donations so that he could purchase a new, $65 million jet in which to travel the world preaching the gospel. The video cited his necessity for the new jet because of mechanical problems with his old jet. Dollar's net worth is a reported $27 million. Now, while most people laughed off the appeal, the real crime was that enough people bought this guy's rap to make him worth $27 million. Then they coughed up the cash and bought him the new jet.

One of the cons these people use to squeeze money out of suckers is the notion that there's a God who's interested in their lives and that, somehow, money is the means of communication. The more you give, the more you get back. It's a testament to our national stupidity about religion that people actually fall for this con. But they do. And have for years. So, let's just clear it up, once and for all.

There is no God who is interested in your life. Jesus doesn't love you because Jesus doesn't know you. He died 2000 years ago and is not coming back because people don't come back from the dead. Jesus doesn't want you to be rich, successful, or happy. Nor does he want you to be poor, homeless, and miserable. That's up to you.

TWENTY-SEVEN

What about all the violence done in the name of religion? What about religious war? Religious war is the greatest oxymoron of all time. Like screwing for virginity. Though I suppose it's a measure of our relative civility in this country that when someone questions our religion, we only get defensive or irate. We don't cut their heads off. Or blow up their cities. My professor in grad school put it very succinctly: "There is no such thing as a religious war. If it's a war, it's not religious."

When the three major religious traditions that share a common philosophical heritage are ready to wipe each other out over a particular patch of dirt, they need to turn inward and examine their understanding of their respective faiths.

Religion has served as a propaganda device for inciting the passions of people with a political grievance and manipulating them into thinking that it's possible, even noble, to kill for God. Although religion is a powerful motivator, ultimately, the human behavior at work is blind belief in any ideology. Stalinist purges, Mao's cultural revolution, the Cambodian killing fields. None of them required religion. What fueled them was blind obedience to some mythical higher calling. It doesn't matter whether it's God, or Dialectical Materialism, Marx's opiate of the masses is also the amphetamine of the extremists.

TWENTY-EIGHT

What about cults? People who are too scared, lazy, or stupid to deal with life as it is often turn to one-size-fits-all belief systems that offer easy answers, and unconditional love. This isn't religion. It's brainwashing and psychological manipulation by greedy, cynical people who prey on human weakness and gullibility.

Scientology is not a religion in any true sense of the word. Despite their billions, they only have tax exempt status because of a 1993 IRS ruling, the result of an avalanche of lawsuits brought by the "church" in a wild attempt to hold off a $1.2 billion tax judgment.

What's also interesting about Scientologists is that they put out this image of being powerful and psychologically grounded yet, when criticized, instantly lapse into raging paranoia. Public denouncements of their critics, hiring private investigators, filing lawsuits -- does this sound like religious behavior? Do you think anything resembling a legitimate religious tradition has something called a "suspicious person?" True religion isn't afraid of criticism. This is the behavior of greedy, power-mad sociopaths.

Also, ask yourself this: when you pass one of the many Scientology outlets in your city, and the sign offers FREE PERSONALITY TESTS, do you think anyone goes in for the test and at the end is told by the auditor: "You're fine. You don't need us. Have a nice day." Doubtful. For the simple reason that it would remove the possibility of turning that person upside-down and shaking out all the money from their pockets. There are only two kinds of people in Scientology: con artists and fools. If you're not one, you're the other.

TWENTY-NINE

What about religious traditions? What about the holidays? Don't they hold the family together and keep traditions alive? Yes, they do. I love Christmastime. But I also know the virgin birth is a myth. You can't make a baby without sex. Easter is a nice time of year. It's spring. People dress nicely. But celebrating a human being coming back from the dead by having parades with people in big hats, after which a man in a bunny suit scatters colored eggs on a lawn for children to find? I don't see the connection.

And, then there's Passover. When I was growing up, every year we were dragged to some relative's house to celebrate the holiday. Although, to us, it was just a bizarre ritual involving a plate of disgusting food, and reading some crazy story that allegedly happened, in reality, some 3500 years ago. But the story made no sense. Frankly, if it were a spec screenplay, there'd be studio notes all over it.

SCREENPLAY SUBMISSION

STUDIO COVERAGE

TITLE: "PASSOVER"

GENRE: BIBLICAL ACTION/DRAMA

SYNOPSIS: JEWISH PEOPLE ARE ENSLAVED IN EGYPT. THEY REVOLT AND ESCAPE.

God places his chosen people in bondage in Egypt. Still, they are fruitful and multiply, until there are so many Jews the Pharaoh is afraid of a revolt.

If God is omnipotent, and loves the Jews, why did He put them in bondage in the first place? Backstory needs clarification, maybe some kind of opening title sequence like in Star Wars. And if He didn't want them to stay in Egypt, why not just pluck them out? If He can create an entire universe, He could certainly send a few ships. It doesn't track. And if this is how He treats His chosen people, it makes you wonder what fate awaits those who weren't chosen. (Just an aside.)

The Pharaoh is so concerned about the rising Jewish population that he decides to be proactive and kill all the first-born Jewish males. Moses' mother and sister place the baby in a basket and send him floating down the river.

No! What if the basket tips over? Babies can't swim. I'm all for dramatic tension but this is child abuse. Recommend some kind of switched at birth, mistaken identity twist. Think Prince and the Pauper. Or Twins. Even something old school like leaving him in a basket on the Pharaoh's doorstep.

The Pharaoh's daughter discovers Moses. He's raised as an Egyptian prince, but years later discovers his true identity, runs off to the desert, gets married, has children, and works as a shepherd. One day, he's told by God, via a burning bush, that he's been chosen to free the Jews from bondage.

The burning bush thing is a bit small. Why not go bigger? A more powerful image. A talking mountain. Or go funny. A talking animal. Like the donkey in Shrek. They had donkeys then, right?

Reluctantly, Moses goes to Pharaoh and says to let his people go. Pharaoh refuses. Moses turns a stick into a snake. Pharaoh's unimpressed. God shows Pharaoh He is not to be trifled with and sends ten plagues: turning water to blood, an infestation of frogs and lice, swarms of flies, rampaging animals, dead livestock, boils, thunder and hail, locusts, and darkness over the land.

Interesting visuals effects, but still feels odd for the God character, given that He's omnipotent. We need a reason for the parlor tricks. Maybe some kind of Superman-type plot device, like Kryptonite, that would weaken Him, and force Him to rely more on his wits. It would inject some dramatic tension while adding dimension to the character, making Him more relatable. I like the "Let my people go" line. Could work for the poster.

Pharaoh still refuses to let the Jews go. God plays the infanticide card and decides to kill all first-born Egyptian sons.

We could probably skate by with one infanticide beat but two is pushing it. It will scare the children and definitely won't play with parents. Maybe God could send a Pied Piper-type messenger to lead the Egyptian kids away to camp or to some Wonka-like chocolate factory. Realize it would change the third act, dramatically, but might be worth considering. (But, seriously, what's the deal with this Biblical penchant for infanticide? From Abraham, who's ready to gut his kid to prove his faith, to God killing his own kid as a morality lesson. Sure, half the time I want to kill my kids, but I'd never actually do it. Sorry, another aside.)

God tells the Jews to slaughter a lamb, then take the blood and mark an "x" over the door of every Jewish household so the Angel of Death will know which houses to "pass over" on his way to killing the Egyptian kids.

The whole Angel of Death character seems unnecessary. Why would an omnipotent God need a hit man? Unless He's so weakened by the Kryptonite device. Still, even the name's melodramatic. The Angel of Death! Plus, I imagine at this point, the lamb's thinking, "Maybe I wouldn't have to die if someone could get their hands on the local phonebook!"

The angel passes over the Jewish houses and kills all the Egyptian kids, including the Pharaoh's. Pharaoh relents and says the Jews can go. So they spring into action and bake bread part way, then pack up and leave. Then the Pharaoh changes his mind and sends his armies after the Jews.

The plot point is unmotivated. Why the Pharaoh's up and back? Doesn't really advance the story in a clever way. Plus, if they knew the whole infanticide thing was coming, why not just start baking bread the night before so it could rise? It feels contrived.

Pharaoh sends his armies after the Jews, who are racing toward the Red Sea.

Ok, this one just stumped me. Even though I know we're heading for the whole Cecil B. DeMille end-of-the-second-act desert chase, no one who's being chased runs <u>toward</u> the sea, unless they know there's a boat waiting. Need a story insight here. Maybe something comedic to explain why they go the wrong way. Might make for a funny character, like the Jewish husband (Billy Crystal) who refuses to ask for directions.

God parts the seas, lets the Jews through, and drowns the Egyptians.

Motivation, motivation, motivation. If the sea hadn't parted yet and they were being chased, how did they know to race toward it? There's no indication they knew this was going to happen. Feels a little Deus Ex Machina.

God has the Jews roam the scorching hot desert with flat bread for 40 years. He gives them a morality lesson by burning a bush and carving some life lessons on two stone tablets, which Moses brings down the mountain but smashes when he sees his people dancing around a giant golden calf.

So, the Jews had no time to let the bread rise yet they were capable of bringing enough gold to melt into a giant calf? Plays into a negative stereotype. We'll get slammed by the media and anti-defamation groups.

The Jews get close to the Promised Land and God tells Moses to check the land He picked out for them. Moses sees it and likes it. Then God kills Moses so he can't go.

Kind of a downer ending. Why not give the hero a win?

Summation: Despite the built-in audience for biblical drama, and the possibilities of strong international box office, the story is convoluted, and filled with plot holes, and character inconsistences.

Recommendation: Pass.

THIRTY

Ok, so now that everybody's offended, let's re-cap: There is no personal God. No King. No Lord. No mysterious creator or ruler of the universe, who loves little children, sends down floods or kills only begotten sons. You don't need God to explain the origin and nature of life. That's a matter for science. You don't need God to establish behavioral guidelines or standards of morality. That's a matter for human reason. You don't need God to give life meaning. Meaning is a man-made concept, something we infer from the experience of being alive. You don't need God to establish that life is good. That's an existential choice.

THIRTY-ONE

So, does this mean that the only stance for an intelligent person on the subject of religion is atheism? Yes. And no. Atheists think they've arrived at the promised land of this argument by rejecting a childish, superstition-based definition of religion. The problem is they don't look any deeper to see if there is a more subtle phenomenon going on, philosophically, and experientially.

Atheism is not the end of the conversation. It's the midway point. For those who call themselves atheists I understand the visceral reaction against anything called religion. Given the way it's discussed and practiced in our lives, and in our history, who can blame them? But the truth is there's a more sophisticated understanding of religion for anyone who cares to look for it.

It says in *I Corinthians 13:11*: *When I was a child, I spake as a child, I understood as a child, I thought as a child. But when I became a man, I put away childish things.* If the goal is to understand the true meaning and purpose of religion, it's time to put away childish things. Atheists are rational, reasonable people. They care about truth, and the truth is that there is a reality-based understanding of religion and religious practice. To understand it, we need to start over.

Anyone who's studied Philosophy knows that any dialogue has to begin by defining one's terms. Otherwise, those involved might as well be speaking different languages. In this case, the enquiry has to begin by asking the basic question: What is religion?

PART TWO

RELIGION

RESURRECTION

*"Experience has repeatedly confirmed
that well-known maxim of Bacon's that
'a little philosophy inclineth a man's mind
to atheism, but depth in philosophy bringeth
men's minds about to religion.'
At the same time when Bacon penned that
sage epigram, he forgot to add that the
God to whom depth in philosophy brings
back men's minds is far from being the same
from whom a little philosophy estranges them."*
George Santayana

THIRTY-TWO

The first step toward arriving at a true understanding of religion is to bring God back down to Earth. Lose the heavens, angels, miracles, afterlife fantasies, creation myths, and magical thinking. Religion is a phenomenon that's based in reality. Despite the proofs for the existence of God put forth by people like Anselm and Augustine, the notion of God as a person is an anthropomorphic holdover from polytheism and a misinterpretation of religious language. And you can't prove the existence of a misinterpretation.

The subject is Philosophy of Religion. The goal is to examine it based on its most intelligent expressions. From a western point of view, the first question in that inquiry is usually: how can there be religion without God? Given the way we've been trained, it's posed as an impossibility. Instead, ask it as a possibility: How can we understand religion without our traditional notion of God?

God is nothing but a word. And words are social conventions used to communicate an idea or experience. Language doesn't denote phenomena; it connotes them. Words are a "finger pointing at the moon." The danger is confusing the finger with what's being pointed at. This is an unusual concept for most of us to grasp because from birth we were fed the notion that religion is based on a God who created everything, who loves me, has plans for my life, and is waiting for me in Heaven. But this is based on the personification of an idea that never should have been personified.

THIRTY-THREE

The next step in deconstructing religion is to remove all the honorific God language: King, King of Kings, Lord, Lord of Lords, Master, Ruler, Creator, Almighty, etc.… And all the personal pronouns: He, His, Who, Thou, Thy, Whom, etc. God is not a person. God does not act. God does not speak. Therefore, there is no one to worship, fear, or pray to. But to say there is no God is not the same as saying god is not real. God is real. But, god, as the word should be understood. Not as a person, but as an experience.

THIRTY-FOUR

Throughout history, mystics from every tradition, whether it was Buddha under the Bodhi tree, Moses on Mt. Sinai, or Jesus or Mohammed in the desert have discovered an experience of human life that is more self-evidently true, good, and beautiful than our normal everyday experience, and they have used the language and philosophical structures of their time to describe it.

Nirvana, Kingdom of Heaven, Tao, Being, Suchness, Buddha, Allah, Brahman, the Great Spirit, nature, or God. Like different words for water in different languages, the words for this phenomenon may vary, but they all point to this single, ultimately real human experience. This is the big bang of all religions. Linguistic and theoretical differences may be interesting from a cultural, historical, or philosophical standpoint, but only after one has understood the singular reality they are intended to express. Philosophers, artists and poets may understand this distinction but the problem is that it hasn't entered the culture. It may seem strange, given our western upbringing, but an impersonal understanding of god is not new in western thought.

"I believe in Spinoza's God who reveals himself in the orderly harmony of what exists,
not in a God who concerns
himself with the fates and actions of human beings…"
Albert Einstein

"Faith consists of being vitally concerned with that ultimate reality to which I give the
symbolical name of God."
Paul Tillich

"We could call order by the name of God, but it would be an impersonal God."
Stephen Hawking

"God is in the world, or nowhere, creating continually in us and around us. Insofar as
man partakes of this creative process does he partake of the divine, of God, and that
participation is his immortality."
Alfred North Whitehead

"All are but parts of one stupendous whole.
Whose body Nature is, and God the soul."
Alexander Pope

"The knower and the known are one. Simple people
imagine they should see God as if he stood there,
and they here. This is not so. God and I,
we are one in knowledge."
Meister Eckhart

"I say to mankind, be not curious about God:
for I, who am curious about each, am not curious about God –
I hear and behold God in every object, yet understand god
not in the least."
Walt Whitman

"I could not say I believe. I know!
I have had the experience of being gripped
by something that is stronger than myself,
something people call God."
Carl Jung

"God is only a great imaginative experience."
D.H. Lawrence

"God is a verb. Not a noun proper or improper,"
Buckminster Fuller

THIRTY-FIVE

To arrive at a more sophisticated understanding of this subject we have to go back to the question: what is religion? Why does the phenomenon exist? What is its intent? What human experience or idea is the word trying to communicate? What need does it fulfill? Why do we have these traditions where, at some point during the week, we stop work and engage in a different activity, whether it's called prayer or meditation? What is its didactic purpose?

The word religion comes from the Latin *re-ligio*, meaning to bind or connect. Like a ligament is a connector. The word *yoga* comes from a Sanskrit word meaning to yoke, and conveys a similar meaning. The purpose of religion is to re-link or re-connect with an experience of life that is beyond our ordinary, everyday, individual experience. Not as an alternative to it, but as an enhancement of it. This awareness, call it spiritual, mystical, or psychological, is the experiential core of all religious traditions.

Religion is an outgrowth of the human desire for self-knowledge, and an experience not just of our common humanity but of our unity with all life. It's the search for enhanced consciousness, higher education in human life. Religion isn't something one believes. It's something one does.

This is the fundamental reason that religion has existed for thousands of years. Within our collective unconscious we know that our ego-driven experience of life is limited. It's like we go through life wearing blinders. If there were not this potential knowledge lurking within us, religion would never have come into existence. The goal is to discern what it is trying to say, not negate it because of its sillier, misguided, or destructive expressions.

THIRTY-SIX

At its heart, religion is the study of the self. It's Socrates' Know Thyself in every sense. From the first moment a baby stares at himself in the mirror and reaches out to touch his face, he begins the process of developing a sense of identity. An "I" that is distinct and separate from the world. This is a matter of survival. But, as that sense of identity becomes more developed, what's lost is the connection with all other things.

The goal of religion is to re-link with that awareness as an adult, to cultivate a renewed sense of wonder. This experience has been called mystical, implying that it's inherently a mystery, but that just demonstrates how divorced from it we've become. In truth, it's simply a matter of a shift in or expansion of one's consciousness and perspective on the world.

THIRTY-SEVEN

"The kingdom of heaven is within you." "He who will drink from my mouth will become like me." Not an actual kingdom. Not an actual drink. This is the metaphorical language of mysticism, used to communicate the nature of a psychological transformation and the path by which individuals can come to it.

But because we're not taught to hear religious language, or to understand myths or symbols, we fall back on simplistic, literal interpretations. This leads to a mindset in which my set of stories and symbols is true; therefore yours are false. This sets religions in opposition to one another—a schism that exists not just between religions but, insanely enough, to sects within traditions.

THIRTY-EIGHT

The purpose of religious myths, iconography, art, symbols and rituals is to lead one to that experience. As Joseph Campbell said: "The purpose of a mythological symbol is to awaken the energies of life." The moment you fall to your knees in front of a cross, thinking you're praying to some God, you're missing the point. The idea is to look through the symbol to the meaning behind it. Or, as Zen Buddhists put it: "If you meet the Buddha on the road, kill him."

THIRTY-NINE

In discussions of religion, the idea of life's meaning comes into play, though to explore the question properly, one has to first step back and define the meaning of "meaning." This is a conversation that usually prompts the uninitiated to scoff about "is the chair really here" philosophy. But, even on the level of conventional conversation, the question that is usually posed is: what is the meaning of life? But it's the wrong question, because it presupposes that meaning is derived from some greater power and has been front-loaded into the system.

The right question is: where is the meaning in life? Meaning is a man-made concept. It's something we infer from those experiences that are self-evidently good, and stem from a feeling of joy and wonder. Meaning is not something that occurs in the future. It exists in the here and now, within the fact that our lives are finite.

FORTY

Prayer and meditation are conscious acts of selflessness. Their purpose is to take one's mind off oneself. To turn off the brain chatter and take a mental break from our everyday concerns. It's about opening one's heart and calming the mind. Per Kierkegaard: "The function of prayer is not to influence god, but rather to change the one who prays."

FORTY-ONE

Religious experience is not about the obliteration of the ego so that one becomes some sort of spineless blob, as some have suggested. Religious insight ultimately involves a synthesis with the ego to form a wiser, more compassionate human being who takes that awareness back into the world. The point of religious life isn't to get something in the future. It's to fully experience the present. That's one difference between religion and the academic tradition. The latter lives in the world of intellectual distinctions but has no built-in path to awareness or transcendence. Academics study the history and philosophy of religion. Monks meditate.

FORTY-TWO

There is a difference between what's true regarding the nature, philosophy and psychology of religion and what is real for most people in their daily lives. The purest form of religious practice may be leading a contemplative life in a monastery, but most people have neither the inclination nor the discipline to do so. We're not all artistically inclined, musically inclined, or spiritually inclined. The world is too much with us. We don't even have anything resembling the Hindu tradition where, after a life of doing one's duty in the world, one retreats to the woods to focus on more spiritual matters. Most people will never have a mystical experience. We're just not wired that way.

Yet within western traditions there is the activity of stepping out of our lives on the Sabbath, going to church on Sunday, or praying five times a day. When we walk in the door of a church, temple, or mosque, we cross a threshold where we leave our normal concerns behind. We put on different clothes. Congregate. Say prayers. There are different sights, smells, sounds, words and music. The purpose is to take one's mind off oneself and open up one's heart. That's the religious intent behind rituals. But when that purpose isn't understood, those rituals descend into rote behavior and obligation, and their true meaning is lost.

FORTY-THREE

Some have suggested that spiritual experience is valuable, but purely as a psychological phenomenon, as Sam Harris wrote in *The End of Faith*. But, this misses the point of religion, which is to affect a psychological transformation in an individual. Saying it's psychological doesn't negate religion, it explains it, as it should be understood. How it's actually understood, however, is another matter entirely.

I am in 99% agreement with the "new atheists" -- Sam Harris and Richard Dawkins most notable among them. It's just at the end of the discussion that I slightly diverge. If the subject is Philosophy of Religion, the point is to accurately define the phenomenon, not reject it because of the words and actions of those who have bastardized it, or used it as a justification for misogyny, homophobia, or murder. At some point, it becomes a semantic discussion, and comes down to agreeing on what one means by "religion."

If you stick with the popular definition that exists in western traditions, one that's based on faith in God, along with all the heinous behavior and belief in fantasy that goes with it, then this psychological experience has absolutely nothing to do with it. That definition is the sad result of a multi-thousand-year-old game of telephone, of smart ideas passed down through stupid people. As Bertrand Russell put it: "A stupid man's report of what a clever man says is never accurate because he unconsciously translates what he hears into something he can understand." Or, to be more charitable, it's what happens when people aren't taught the intent of the language and symbols, and about the subtlety of the ideas being expressed.

If, however, you re-define religion as a system of symbols, practices, and rituals intended to guide one toward that experience, then you can work out from there and reach a new appreciation of it. At this point, some have argued that if spirituality is essentially a psychological phenomenon, ultimately there's no need for traditional religions, with all their concomitant mythological and homicidal baggage. That may be true, but I don't see how this argument will suddenly, and magically make these traditions disappear. We are where we are, so we might as well deal with the situation as it is.

FORTY-FOUR

Another reason for not damning the entirety of religion is more pragmatic, even tactical. Those who pride themselves on being believers will ultimately reject any argument made by atheists on the basis that they just don't respect religion, or think it's important. Even the most civilized among them will land on "let's just agree to disagree." The stronger argument is to respond, "I do think that religion is important. I just don't think you understand the very religion you hold so dear." In the best of all possible worlds, this knocks them off their axis, and opens them up to take a more critical look at their own assumptions.

FORTY-FIVE

It is also unfair, and inaccurate to condemn the totality of religion based on the aberrant, selfish, hypocritical behavior of those who have talked the talk, but not walked the walk. Financial improprieties, sexual misconduct -- there have been numerous offenders throughout history, and right up to the present. Absolute power can corrupt, absolutely. And absolute religious power can be an even more seductive drug. It's not surprising that many have used it for less than charitable purposes. But this conflict is fundamental to religion. Its battleground is the human heart and the eternal struggle between our better natures and our selfish desires. Religion exists in the world of this conflict, not outside it.

FORTY-SIX

You could erase the names of every religious figure in history, destroy every book, symbol, building and artifact from every tradition known to man, but you still couldn't eliminate the religious impulse, because it's imbedded in our collective unconscious. Despite the aberrant behavior that currently defines much of western religion, each tradition has had its respective spiritual renaissance: Christian Gnostics, Sufi mystics, Kabbalah in Judaism. To the extent that these traditions thrive, religion remains alive inside Religion.

Even though the core truth of religion has been buried under centuries of misconceptions, miscommunication, literal interpretations of symbolic language, fear, greed, stupidity, and lack of proper education, every tradition has within its framework a path toward the same transcendent experience. But as long as the discussion remains mired in silly arguments between faith and reason, religion and science, or belief and atheism, we will never crawl out of this intellectual hole we've dug for ourselves.

FORTY-SEVEN

So, if that's what religion is, what do I do about it? That depends. You don't have to do anything. The point is just to understand it, to elevate the level of the conversation. When I first began studying this subject 45 years ago, devouring every book I could get my hands on, I did so with the assumption that my study came with some sort of behavioral imperative. That once I figured out the truth I would have to change my life accordingly and follow that path. Young people tend to think in such absolute terms.

But if Socrates' Know Thyself has any meaning, it's on two levels: to come to know your essential self, and to accept your existential self. The latter is an awareness that can come with maturity and thinking over time. But even when I was younger I knew in my heart that I was too caught up in the things of this world to run off to a monastery. I still am. It just doesn't fit my temperament. Not to say I haven't tried to incorporate what I've discovered into my thinking, and my life as much as possible.

FORTY-EIGHT

So, maybe you're not buying any of this. You were raised to believe in God and believe in God is what you're going to do. Besides, what's wrong with having faith? The answer is nothing. People have the right to believe anything they want. That's the way we do things here. Some people just want comfort, and they're not going to look any further, probe any deeper, or think any harder.

When I published my book, I sent it to the Religion editor of a popular news website. He was also a professor of Religion at a prestigious east coast university. When we spoke, I asked him what he thought. He tactfully replied, "at least I know where you stand." I tried to continue the conversation, making my arguments, when he cut me off, saying, "You'll never convince me there's no God." So, that was that. At least I knew where he stood. Conversation over. Which was fine.

If the traditional belief in God is what feels right to you, if it orders your life, gives you an identity, makes you feel grounded, helps you deal with suffering, does no harm, and comforts you with the feeling that your departed loved ones are with Jesus or in God's loving embrace and that you will see them one day in the afterlife, then I say go with God, in every sense. Go with your own interpretation. And go in peace.

For those who are so put off by every ignorant, hateful thing that has been done in the name of religion, it may be too difficult to look at the phenomenon with new eyes. Which is fine. As long as you live a decent, ethical life, then go without God. At the end of the day, it's about what gets you through the night.

FORTY-NINE

While mystical experience may be the experiential core of religion, the larger practice of religion involves our behavior in the world: Love, compassion, tolerance, charity, patience, forgiveness. These are not just the buzzwords of a Sunday sermon, but the values we should live by. Both religious and secular intellectual traditions end up in this same place.

In the end there are only two kinds of people: those who want to live their lives and experience all the joy they can for themselves and others, and those who want to bring harm into the world. It's the purpose of religion to bring comfort to the former, not fuel the destructive impulses of the latter.

FIFTY

The main thing wrong with religion is that people have gotten it wrong. The goal is to understand religion as it should be understood, as traditions, myths, symbols, and practices intended to lead one to a deeper, more profound experience of human life. The desire for this knowledge is hard wired in us. That won't disappear. Unless of course we wipe each other out in the next holy war, in which case we've successfully screwed ourselves.

CHAPTER NINE

DUMBF⬛CK HABITS

SMOKING: A MEMOIR

"To me, a cigarette is food."
Frank Zappa

Obviously you're still reading, and not totally pissed off about the whole "no God" thing. Or the "there's actually a deeper meaning to religion" thing. So, let's lighten things up and talk about smoking. Maybe you're wondering why a chapter on smoking is relevant in a book about our dumb culture. The answer is this: there's nothing dumber than smoking. Nothing.

People overeat but we all have to eat. People drink too much, but we all have to drink. We don't all have to drink alcohol, but it's not that big a leap. No one has to take a dried-out plant that's been laced with Formaldehyde, arsenic, ammonia, DDT, Carbon Monoxide and 43 other carcinogenic chemicals, roll it into a long, paper cylinder, set it on fire, and suck hot, toxic smoke into their lungs 20 times a day. Not to mention addicting yourself to a poison that clogs your arteries, shortens your life, leaves a dank, putrid smell on your breath, hands, clothes, hair, spouse, house, pets and children, pisses off everyone around you, and turns you into a social pariah.

Nor does it do wonders for your appearance. Actress Bette Davis was a lifetime smoker. Even late in life, she reportedly smoked 5 packs a day. At the end, before she died of cancer, she looked like a stick of beef jerky in a wig. The Rolling Stones, apparently due to a deal with the devil, look like cigarettes that have been left standing on a table to burn down. Yet, they're still going strong, for which I, as a Stones' fan, am personally grateful. At this point, Keith Richards may actually be 80% nicotine.

There is no more pathetic sight than people standing around sucking that shit into their lungs. They're like throwbacks to a bygone era. Or you'd think it was bygone. Despite the warnings on cigarettes packs that smoking will kill you, 41 million Americans still smoke. Why? Because we're a bunch of dumb, stubborn dumbfucks.

Though we're not the dumbest. 29% of Europeans smoke. But somehow they look cool doing it, especially the French. Like characters in a Truffaut film. (Francois Truffaut, iconic French film director. My favorite: *Day for Night, 1973.*) Same for the Italians, (Fellini, *8 ½, 1963.*) Almost 20% of Japanese still smoke, yet almost none of them look cool doing it. The least cool are the Russians. It seems they all smoke. Though maybe when you live in Russia, early death is less of a tragedy and more of a reprieve. Yet, here in America, where anyone under the age of 70 has had it drummed into their head from birth that cigarettes are lethal, we're still at it. Still, why a chapter on smoking? Because smoking, as well as trying to quit, are emblematic of the American mindset in three ways.

<u>ONE</u>

<u>PERSONAL FREEDOM</u>

We Americans take pride in the fact that we have the freedom to do whatever we want. That includes smoking ourselves to death. (Of course, when cigarettes give us cancer and we're wasting away, it's usually those same freedom-lovers who don't think we should have the right to end our lives. We can commit slow suicide. Just not quickly at the end.)

And while there are restrictions on that freedom in order to mitigate the harmful effects of secondhand smoke, we don't care. We'll light up wherever we can. We'll even go in those airport terrariums. Bunch of sad bastards milling around like contestants in an isolation booth in some '50s game show, or a diorama at the Museum of Natural History. Primitive man. Maybe one day they'll replace the exhibit of cavemen holding spears with a group of smokers. *Homo Fumeus.* Extinct.

TWO

CORPORATE FREEDOM

Tobacco companies have the right to manufacture and sell an addictive poison. And given the counterintuitive nature of their business, in which they are simultaneously serving and annihilating their customer base, they can also market it to new generations using every trick at their disposal.

I grew up with cigarette commercials. TV shows sponsored by Old Gold and Lucky Strike. Leggy dancers inside cigarette pack costumes selling the notion that smoking is sexy. Even when, after years of tobacco company stonewalling, TV cigarette ads were banned in 1971, the companies still got their message out. In 2010, the combined profit of the six major tobacco companies was $35.1 billion. In 2012 they spent over $9 billion on advertising and promotion.

I worked in advertising in the '80s in New York. A friend of mine worked at McCann Erickson, marketing Joe Camel -- a hip-looking character wearing shades, with a butt hanging out of his mouth -- sort of a mashup of James Dean and Joe Cool. And what's cooler than knowing you're killing yourself and not giving a shit? My friend was torn. He didn't like what he was doing, but a job was a job. He was also a former smoker. He died years later of a heart attack.

Even when cigarette companies were prevented from lying overtly, they stalled any regulation by creating a smokescreen of doubt about the health risks. In 1994 the presidents and CEOs of the seven largest tobacco companies went before a congressional committee and swore that nicotine was not addictive. We've learned a few things since then. Or maybe we haven't.

A 2015 study by the Center for Environmental Health found evidence that e-cigarettes contain cancer-causing agents. A report by the CDC stated that use of electronic cigarettes among teenagers has tripled over the last year. RJ Reynolds is in the vaping business. A recent issue of *Rolling Stone* featured a Newport cigarettes ad on the inside cover, with a picture of a young, hip band; an ad for blu PLUS+ e-cigs, with a smiling young girl with arm tattoos; and a double-page spread for mint-flavored Copenhagen smokeless tobacco. One way or another, they're going to make a buck off people sucking in nicotine.

THREE

HOW WE QUIT

      While we tend to acknowledge our responsibility in taking up the habit, we think we're powerless when it comes to quitting. We assume the only way to do it is via some outside agent that will remove the devil from our bodies, like a nicotine exorcism. That's why we reach for any product we're told will do the trick: Patches. Gum. Pills. A popular product advertising on TV is Chantix. According to its website, Chantix is "a prescription medication that, along with support, helps adults 18 and over stop smoking." Also from its website, this important safety information:

Some people have had changes in behavior, hostility, agitation, depressed mood, suicidal thoughts or actions while using CHANTIX to help them quit smoking. Some people had these symptoms when they began taking CHANTIX, and others developed them after several weeks of treatment or after stopping CHANTIX. If you, your family or caregiver notice agitation, hostility, depression or changes in behavior, thinking, or mood that are not typical for you, or you develop suicidal thoughts or actions, anxiety, panic, aggression, anger, mania, abnormal sensations, hallucinations, paranoia or confusion, stop taking CHANTIX and call your doctor right away. Also tell your doctor about any history of depression or other mental health problems before taking CHANTIX, as these symptoms may worsen while taking CHANTIX. Some people had seizures during treatment with CHANTIX. Most cases happened during the first month of treatment. Tell your doctor if you have a history of seizures. If you have a seizure during treatment with CHANTIX, stop taking CHANTIX and contact your healthcare provider right away. Decrease the amount of alcohol you drink while taking CHANTIX until you know if CHANTIX affects your ability to tolerate alcohol. Some people experienced increased drunkenness, unusual or sometimes aggressive behavior, or memory loss of events while consuming alcohol during treatment with CHANTIX. Do not take CHANTIX if you have had a serious allergic or skin reaction to CHANTIX. Some people can have serious skin reactions while taking CHANTIX, some of which can become life-threatening. These can include rash, swelling, redness, and peeling of the skin. Some people can have allergic reactions to CHANTIX, some of which can be life-threatening and include: swelling of the face, mouth, and throat that can cause trouble breathing. If you have these symptoms or have a rash with peeling skin or blisters in your mouth, stop taking CHANTIX and get medical attention right away. Before starting CHANTIX, tell your doctor if you have a history of heart or blood vessel problems. If you have new or worse heart or blood vessel symptoms during treatment, tell your doctor. Get emergency medical help right away if you have any symptoms of a heart attack or stroke. The most common side effects of CHANTIX include nausea (30%), sleep problems, constipation, gas and/or vomiting. If you have side effects that bother you or don't go away, tell your doctor. You may have trouble sleeping, vivid, unusual or strange dreams while taking CHANTIX. Use caution driving or operating machinery until you know how CHANTIX may affect you. CHANTIX should not be taken with other quit-smoking products. You may need a lower dose of CHANTIX if you have kidney problems or get dialysis. Before starting CHANTIX, tell your doctor if you are pregnant, plan to become pregnant, or if you take insulin, asthma medicines or blood thinners. Medicines like these may work differently when you quit smoking."

So, you can be pretty sure it's safe.

We view quitting smoking the same way we view diets, exercise regimens, and religions. They're external forces that we, the passive users, employ to work their magic on us. Just follow the directions. And if one device or method doesn't work, try another. Because just as with diets, exercise regimens, and religions, we think the variable is the method, not the person.

We succumb to the habit because we're susceptible to images. Our difficulty in quitting reveals that same passivity. We're always looking for the magic bullet that will cure us. Our freedom to indulge in a lethal habit got us hooked and our approach to quitting keeps us hooked. As opposed to realizing that <u>we</u> started this, so <u>we</u> need to end it.

And I say this not as a critic or outside observer, but as an 18-year smoker who was absolutely convinced I was immune to the harmful effects of smoking. Yes, I am capable of that degree of self-delusion. To this day, I don't know what possessed me. I hated smoking. Then I loved smoking. And once I was hooked, I had no desire to quit, until I had to. That's when I stumbled on a way to do it that had nothing to do with any product. That's the reason for this chapter. I want to pass on what I discovered. Because it's a method I've never heard anyone suggest in quite this way.

Maybe you smoke and want to quit. Maybe you know someone who does. Either way, this worked for me and it's a potential way out of the habit that avoids the pitfalls, head games, and torture of giving up something you've grown to love and depend on. But first, my smoking history.

MY SMOKING HISTORY

    I smoked my first cigarette when I was 12. At the time I remember thinking it was really cool, though looking back I can't remember what possessed me to try it. Maybe it was the cartons of unfiltered Luckys and Chesterfields my parents had stashed in a kitchen drawer. Maybe it was the cigarette commercials on TV, or the movie icons. Humphrey Bogart. Steve McQueen. James Dean. They all looked so hip with that butt dangling off their lips.

    All I know is some friends and I decided that smoking was something we needed to check out. Somehow, we got our hands on a pack of menthols, and began lighting up on the walk to school. We took a route that went through the woods above the community park. We'd cleverly stash our packs in a hollow tree, and then retrieve them on the way home. I have no idea how our teachers or parents didn't smell it on us. But they didn't. It was my first experiment with cigarettes, my first flirtation with cool. But it didn't last. Maybe it was the fact that I started playing soccer and needed the lung power. But for some reason, the allure wore off as quickly as that first head rush, and I just left it behind.

    I didn't smoke all through high school. Neither did my friends. Even when we started getting high, which was senior year, it never transitioned into smoking cigarettes. Besides, if my parents had smelled it on me they would've killed me. My mother had quit by then. My father did as well. Though, years later, he took it up again, smoking these little cigarette-like cigars that came in a Dunhill-style green and black box. I can still see that box on the kitchen table, next to his silver lighter, when he'd light up after dinner. Smoking at the dinner table, in the house, with the kids around. This was the late '60s. Nobody had a problem with that. He died of a heart attack a few years later at 44.

    College as well was a non-smoking affair. By that time, cigarettes had become repugnant to me. My freshman roommate smoked Marlboros. Once, during a massive snowstorm, we were stranded in the dorms. All the roads were closed. As a joke, I held his last cigarette between my fingers and threatened to break it against his chest. He dared me to do it. So I did. And we laughed. Looking back, from the vantage point of a long-time smoker, I would have thrown me out the 10th floor window.

    My sophomore roommate used to wake up at the crack of noon in a complete fog, fall out of bed, and crawl across the floor looking for his ashtray, like a newborn puppy searching for his mother's nipple. Then he'd carefully straighten out the largest butt he could find, fire it up, and inhale his first drag along with his first breath.

    Dope aside, I got through four years of undergraduate work without a single cigarette. Same for grad school, where I lived like a monk, in a math professor's basement, with a cat that would bring me a field mouse for breakfast every morning. Even after receiving a Dear John letter from my college girlfriend on the same day I got a notice from the university cutting my scholarship, I didn't run to light up. If ever the table was set for taking up cigarettes, or heroin, it was then. But I didn't. It just never entered my mind. You'd think making it all the way to 24 without smoking would have rendered me too smart to start. Not so.

After completing my course work, I went to Kyoto, Japan to research my Master's thesis on Buddhism. Everyone smoked in Japan -- men, women, kids, dogs, cats. We used to hang out in *kisatens* – small, pre-Starbucks coffee shops that served this exquisite, rich, steamed coffee. Young Japanese kids would read *manga* (Japanese comic books), drink coffee, and smoke their brains out. Friday nights in the traditional *Gion* district was a cacophonous, moveable drunken feast of inebriated businessmen, cigarettes dangling precariously from their lips, as they staggered down the street, stopping only to puke in the gutter. Even the Geisha in their flowery kimono would gracefully stroll through the back alleys, daintily puffing on cigarettes.

Eventually, I quit my degree program, and got jobs teaching English, while continuing to study Japanese. I taught in schools, as well as privately. I made some friends but, overall, I was bored, and lonely -- a recently jilted ex-pat with a ton of free time and no one to kill it with. I'd walk the banks of the *Kamogawa* – the river that runs through Kyoto -- see the couples strolling hand in hand, and feel like a stowaway on Noah's Ark. (Not the real ark. That didn't exist. The metaphorical ark where everyone's paired up.)

One day, while hanging out in a building lobby, waiting for a student, I found myself standing next to a cigarette machine. And the thought just popped into my head. Why not buy a pack? Might help pass the time. Then I thought, oh right, these things are lethal. Then I thought, screw it. A few cigarettes won't kill me. I'm 24. I'm immortal.

I decided I would stick my hand in my pocket and if I had enough change to buy a pack, I would. If not, I wouldn't. Nothing like leaving a life and death decision up to fate. I stuck my hand in my pocket, and pulled out a massive handful of *Yen*. And that was it. I put the coins in the machine, checked out the brands, and decided on a pack of *Lucky 7s*. It was the old-fashioned kind of machine, where you punched in the number of your choice, and yanked out the handle as the pack dropped down with a gallows-like thud. Even that death metaphor didn't stop me. I think some matches came with it. Fate's way of making sure I wouldn't change my mind.

I took the pack and instantly liked the feel of it. Like shaking hands with a new friend. I removed the plastic, taking in that first tobacco whiff. I carefully tore out a corner, tapped the side against my palm, and popped out my first adult cigarette. I stuck it in my mouth, tasting the asbestos-y filter against my tongue. Then I lit it, took a long drag, and got that first nauseating, woozy head rush. Your body's way of saying, "What the fuck?! What is that?! What are you doing?! Stop that, you asshole! Stop it!"

I was nauseous. Queasy. But, still pressed on with the experiment. I took another drag, and walked around the block, blending into the crowd. Well, as well as any *gaijin* could blend in, in Japan. I finished the cigarette, flicked it on the street, stamped it out, and lit another. This was great. I liked the feeling that I was no longer doing nothing. I had an activity to pass the time.

Next thing I remember was waking up in my tiny apartment, and seeing the pack on the night table. No matter how alone I'd been I wasn't lonely anymore. My new friends were with me. A week later I was up to a pack a day. Hooked.

I smoked my way through the Japanese brands, like Seven Stars and Peace. Via some ex-pats I knew, I also flirted with Dunhills, *Gitanes*, and *Gauloise*. It was a wide, wide world of smoking, and I loved it all. The street malls in Kyoto sold these slick, cheap, electric lighters. You popped the top with your thumb and flicked the wheel on the side, which sent up a cool, blue flame. Leaning against a building, I'd stick a butt in my mouth, flick the lighter, light up, take a drag, and slowly exhale, as I'd watch the people pass by. Cigarettes weren't just my new friends; they were my new, cool friends.

After 8 months, I decided the ex-pat life wasn't for me. I wasn't going to shave my head and enter a monastery, like the Canadian guy I met. And my visa was running out. So, I left and went home to New York, crashing with my mother on Long Island until I could finagle my way into the city. She was disappointed that I'd taken up smoking, but she didn't complain when I selfishly stunk up her apartment. She was going through her own tough times having divorced her second husband, so a little acrid tobacco smoke was the least of her worries.

I hung out, watched TV, smoked, and occasionally hit the bars, where my new friends came in handy, removing the need for a clever opening line. You could just walk up to some girl in a bar or disco, ask for a light or to bum a cigarette, and take it from there. Well, theoretically you could, except this was 1977, the Summer of Sam, and women looked at every guy like he could be the .44 Caliber killer. No one was going home with anyone. Like it wasn't hard enough to meet women, having no job, no car, no money, and living with my mother. Now I had to prove I wasn't a psycho killer.

After freeloading for a few months, I finally realized I had to get off my ass and look for work. So, I put on my only suit – a horrible, grey pinstriped monstrosity – and, armed with *The New York Times* Help Wanted section, took the train into the city.

There's no word to describe the fetid wave of urban stench that hits you when you climb the stairs and exit Penn Station onto 7th Avenue on a hot, summer morning -- cabs belching fumes, buses lumbering by, farting out noxious exhaust. It was hot, grimy, humid and depressing. Thinking of the daunting task ahead, my heart would sink. But then I'd remember I wasn't alone. My friends were with me. I'd take out the pack, tap out a butt, light up, and take a drag. Then, with newfound resolve, I'd hit the employment agencies, all of which, despite the promising ads for exciting careers in publishing or advertising, were just looking for smart, cute, college-educated women to hire as secretaries. Hard to believe my Philosophy degree, travel experience, basic writing ability, and erratic 50-words-per-minute typing skills didn't open the doors to opportunity. I hiked all over Manhattan that summer, searching for a job, with no luck. But at least my cigarettes were on the journey with me, Don Quixote tilting at windmills, along with his carcinogenic Sancho Panza.

A couple months later I bought my way into a studio apartment on 2nd Avenue and 80th, and resumed the hunt, eventually landing jobs at a cheese shop, sleazy magazine company, porn magazine, travel marketing company, and an ad agency. I met a girl and we moved in together with her daughter. I was still happily smoking. My future mother-in-law was a health nut who swore by various nutrition gurus she would listen to on the radio. She also smoked two packs of long, thin 100mm cigs a day. She died of cancer.

The only thing better than smoking was smoking in the city. The walk-to-the-train cigarette. The ride-the-subway cigarette. The walk-to-the-office cigarette. The ride-up-the-elevator cigarette. The phone call cigarette. The meeting cigarette. The walk home cigarette. The stop-in-a-bar-for-a-drink-on-the-way-home cigarette. The get home cigarette. Before dinner. After dinner. In bed. The 3 a.m. dark night of the soul cigarette. What are you going to do: stare out the window and ponder the meaning of life with a cup of chamomile tea?

And if this didn't tempt fate enough, despite my family history, in which the men all died before 50, my diet featured meat, butter, eggs, hot dogs, fast food burgers, and fries. If there was no meat in it, it wasn't a meal. As well, I started drinking way too much. And doing cocaine recreationally. I would have done it habitually, but I couldn't afford it. I even smoked while playing soccer in a league with a bunch of waspy, Upper West Siders. I smoked before the game. Smoked during. Smoked after. And I didn't see a doctor for 10 years. My way of staring death in the face and saying: "Cigarettes? Unhealthy lifestyle? Family history? You can't touch me! I'm immortal!"

At that time, I started writing jokes for comics, as well as spec TV and movie scripts. And I discovered an even deeper relationship with my friends – the writing cigarette. There's no single image more implanted on a writer's mind than the typewriter, ashtray, and pack of butts nearby. It wasn't just the writing cigarette. It was the writing break cigarette, the thinking cigarette, the walk-around-the-block-to-clear-your-head cigarette. Even when you were stuck, cigarettes were a calming, reassuring voice, saying, "Don't worry, man. Just light up, we'll figure it out."

Smoking got me through about seven years of odd jobs, while taking exploratory trips to L.A. to test the show business waters. By this time I'd grown less enchanted with flying. It took a few cigs, and two Bloody Marys in the airport just to get me on a 9 a.m. flight. But the second we were wheels up and that "no smoking" sign pinged off, I'd grab my pack and light up. And it was all good. Two more Bloodys on the plane and five more cigs and I'd make it through to landing, when I'd intone the secret touchdown mantra I've used for 30 years: "survived another one."

Finally, I optioned a movie script, which lead to a re-write on a genuine Hollywood studio movie, which got rolled into a one-year overall deal. So, I packed up my family, typewriter, cat, and cigarettes, and moved out to Los Angeles, where I immediately discovered a brand new smoking moment: the driving cigarette. This was hardly the same as the back-of-the-cab cigarette. Most New York cabs smelled like a wet ashtray. That, combined with the cliché *French Connection* ride through traffic, and you were lucky if you didn't self-immolate just trying to light up.

My first L.A. car was a cool, black '86 Mustang convertible. I'd hit the button, sending the rag top easing into the back, then turn on the radio or stick in a cassette. (Cassettes were what we used to listen to music after albums, which were then replaced by CDs. CDs were what we used before it all went digital. Digital was how we listened before people rediscovered albums, only now they're called vinyl. Everything old is new again.)

Anyway, I'd light up, take a drag, and pull into traffic. No matter what song came on, in my head it was Randy Newman's "I Love L.A." Over the years, I drove a convertible Alfa, and a Porsche. Same joy. Pop the top, light up a smoke, and drive down Sunset. Life couldn't get any better. Even when you're cutting it short.

This was in the mid '80s, and if the country was on a health kick, you wouldn't know it by me. I stubbornly kept smoking into my mid 30s. I worked with smokers. Smoked at all my jobs. Nothing stopped me. Not even a heart attack scare in my late 30s that turned out to be just a panic attack, but still came with an ambulance ride to UCLA Medical. Once I was given the all clear, I went home, took a deep breath, and lit up. That was the best smoke of all -- the defiant I-just-cheated-death cigarette. And so it went. Until I hit my late 30s and went to a doctor for the first time in over 15 years.

It may have been at my brother's urging, as he was a non-smoker and never stopped giving me shit about my filthy habit. Maybe it was our family history. In any event, he recommended his doctor in Beverly Hills. I figured why not. Other than a few emergency room visits over the years for sports injuries, and arthroscopic knee surgery, I hadn't had a check up. No blood tests. Pee tests. Chest x-ray. Nothing. Couldn't hurt.

So, I went to the doctor. Very cool guy. A smoker. He did the exam, and ran the usual tests. Then we sat in his office, lit up, and discussed the results. They were not good. My cholesterol was over 300. My blood may have been half motor oil. He prescribed some pills, told me to change my diet, exercise, and, given my family history, quit smoking. I pointed out that he was smoking when he said that. He replied, "My life is none of your business. Quit. Or die."

I did not like that. I did not like that one bit. Not the test results, but the fact that I had to quit smoking. Who the hell was this guy to take away my friends? My writing friends, my walking friends, my driving friends, my after-sports friends, my middle-of-the-night friends. Hell, I came from New York and was living in L.A. The pollution was probably killing me.

I'm stubborn. I don't like to admit it, being stubborn and all. But I am. Still, I'm not stupid. Check that. I've done some incredibly stupid things in my life, all the while thinking I knew exactly what I was doing. Like taking up smoking. But it finally occurred to me that maybe I should begin to consider entertaining the thought that, being a doctor and all, the guy might know what he's talking about. So I took a shot and quit cold turkey. And it worked. For 35 days. During which time I turned into such an ornery bastard that my wife said, "Oh, for fuck sake, just smoke already." Which was all I needed to hear. So, I had one. Then another. Then, after a few days, with those test results safely fading into the past, I took it as the all clear to resume smoking. My friends and I were back together. Reunited.

By the way, one reason cold turkey is a lousy way to quit is that you're trying to purge an addiction you've had for years in one big move. You're slamming into a brick wall at 60 mph, instead of pumping the brakes to slow down. The pack-a-day urge is still there. Twenty times a day your body's going, "Feed me, you bastard, feed me!" Even if you can tough it out, you can't immediately lose all the psychological crutches. All those special moments are gone. And it's hell living without them. It's a break up. You're pining for your friends. You want them back. But you know they're not coming back. It's like there's a Hank Williams song playing in your head, all day long. You're sad, anxious, pissed off. And what do you do when you're sad, anxious, and pissed off? You smoke.

That's when the head games start. You think, "Oh, hell. I've gone without cigarettes for a few days. I can do this. I'm kicking it. I'll just have one, what could it hurt?" So you light up. And it's amazing. Like a midnight "I miss you" call that leads to a tearful reunion, make-up sex, and the promise to "never let anything come between us again." Then you have another. And another. Until your inner addict says, "Screw it, we can't do this. Give it up. Keep smoking." Unless you've got a will of iron, cold turkey is a bitch.

At that time I was working in television, and you could light up in a writers' room, as well as on stage. One night we worked until 4:30 a.m. rewriting a script. Seven of us sitting in a windowless room, smoking this one poor bastard out to the point that his eyes were so bloodshot he looked like a very sad bald eagle.

After that job ended, I got on a Paramount show called *Wings*. That's where my education in quitting began. Things were different. It was a non-smoking room. For a while you could smoke on stage but eventually they banned that, too. And fewer people smoked. It was just two of us. The office was on the second floor, so we'd have to keep running downstairs to light up outside. And that became a problem.

Writing on a TV show is mostly group work. Sitting in a room for hours breaking stories or punching up scripts. There's a flow to the day and you can't keep running out of the room every thirty minutes for a cigarette. You'll start getting looks from people. Plus you stink when you get back. And my goal at that point was to not stink.

So, as a matter of necessity, when the nicotine pang hit me, I'd have to tough it out, knowing I could give in to the next one. So, that's what I did. When it came on, I'd acknowledge it, resist it, and let it pass, which it did. And it was tolerable because I knew I could satisfy it later, which I did. But then I'd only have one, not two or three to make up for the missed ones.

That's when an unexpected thing happened. I noticed that, by the end of the day, I still had a few cigarettes left in the pack. As a pack-a-day smoker, that usually wasn't the case. I soon realized what was going on. By riding out the urges I was smoking less. Not that I saw it as a way to quit but, in and of itself, smoking less was fine. And now that I knew I could control it, it became a challenge to see how many urges could I pass up without giving in. I'd test myself to see how tough I was. How long I could go. Again, it was all made easier knowing I could give in any time and smoke. Without realizing it, I was slowly detoxing.

This was different from using gum or a patch. I wasn't getting my nicotine from another source. I was expunging it from my system and getting my body used to less. I was quitting, while smoking. And I was in control. I wasn't losing my friends all at once. They were always there whenever I wanted them. I kept smoking, but smoking less and less.

That's when the idea of quitting really started to kick in. It wasn't an intellectual realization as much as a reduction in the cravings. My body just didn't want it as much. I was slowly reverting to my pre-smoking condition. I wasn't fighting an overwhelming urge twenty times a day. I was experiencing fewer urges. My body was cleansing the poison from my system. The less I took in, the less I wanted. I kept tapering off for a couple years, until I was down to a few cigarettes a day. And even those I could take or leave. But I still hung onto the habit, not ready to completely let go.

Around that time I'd reached my early forties, and several things happened in my life that were, well, life-changing. My mother had been diagnosed with colon cancer. After an operation and some chemo she moved out to L.A., where she found an apartment in Beverly Hills. She got a job, and tried to carve out a new life. But then the cancer returned. Even several years of chemo couldn't kill it. Then one day her doctor said there was nothing more he could do. We went back to her apartment, and sat around the table, when suddenly she looked up and said, "Why is everything blue?" Then she collapsed. We carried her to bed, and called the hospice workers, who arrived and set up a morphine drip. That began a three-day vigil with my immediate family and some relatives. Then she passed away.

The second life-altering event was the birth of my daughter. While I had been a stepparent for years, I'd never experienced the moment of holding your newborn child in your arms. This injected me with something I hadn't felt in years: the will to live. Not that I'd wanted to die, exactly. It's just that I kept tempting fate to the point where I felt it was going to bitchslap me back. And now I didn't want it to.

The other thing that occurred to me was that it probably wasn't great parenting to stink of cigarettes every time you picked up your kid. And it wasn't practical to shower after every smoke, or put on a Hazmat suit just to read *Pat the Bunny* at bedtime. And I guess a case could be made that second-hand smoke is bad for infants. This is when I got it in into my head that maybe I should start thinking about considering the possibility of quitting completely. I didn't. But I did continue my program of cutting down, while smoking. By now it was a thing I did once in a while, as opposed to habitually. As well, I realized I was coughing less.

I forgot to mention that other aspect of my smoking habit: the cough. I had a ridiculous, constant, throat-clearing, phlegm-rattling hack that I absolutely refused to admit had anything to do with smoking. Yes, I am capable of that degree of self-delusion. It's sort of gone now. Though a more -- and I shudder to use the word – benign version of the throat-clearing thing is still there. Along with my sinuses, which are as clogged as the 405 Freeway on a Monday morning, just a little souvenir from 18 years of cigarettes.

I kept cutting down until I was only smoking a few cigarettes a week. As well, all the habitual moments were gone. I could write without them. Play sports without them. Drive without them. Then, one day… I just stopped. I didn't consciously quit. My body just didn't want any more nicotine. I liked the way not smoking felt. I stopped buying cigarettes. I didn't bum any. I was done. After 18 years, I was now a non-smoker. And had no desire to pick it up again.

And it lasted… about three years. Until the day my entire house was flooded with sewage, courtesy of a clogged city line. It was the same day a show I'd created premiered on NBC to disappointing ratings and crappy reviews. That night, while talking to the guys in the street who were unclogging the line, I bummed a smoke. It was the first cigarette I'd had in years. And it was good. Like re-uniting with an old friend.

It started me back on the road to chipping one or two a day. Maybe even three. An occasional writing cigarette, or drink cigarette. Soon after I started on another Paramount show – *Becker*. It was also a non-smoking room, although a few of us would duck out after lunch or at night during a long re-write and light up. And it was fun. But I never went back to a pack a day. I had detoxed to the point that my body didn't want it. The thought of sucking in that much smoke was repugnant. But chipping a few every day was an amusing little diversion.

Not a habit. I played with that for a few more years. Nothing wrong with the occasional cigarette, or so I told myself.

Finally, I think it was when I returned home after my last studio deal ended, I completely gave it up. I was still smoking a few a week, but having to deal with the residual stench from just one became annoying. Although I'd been exercising off and on for at least ten years, I began to do it daily. I liked the feeling of breathing in oxygen, or L.A.'s version of it. I felt clean. And cigarettes were dirty. Finally, the last residual urges faded away and I was done. Out clean. I was a non-smoker. I had quit.

I haven't touched a cigarette in about 10 years, and have no desire to smoke. The thought of drawing that noxious shit into my lungs nauseates me just as it did before I started. Occasionally, I'll catch some fumes from someone smoking on the street, and enjoy the quick, nostalgic rush, but it doesn't make me want to start again. Like bumping into an old girlfriend and appreciating the fact that she still looks good, but not really wanting to hook up again.

So, that's the trick. You detox slowly, powering through as many craving moments as you can before having one. This way you don't have to experience the sudden emotional loss of your friends. You don't have the cold turkey body shock. You don't have the "I can't do this" mind trick every time you give in and have one, so that you instantly give up on quitting. You smoke and quit at the same time. You detox slowly. You also learn to break those old habits as you purge the drug from your system, and if you can start exercising at the same time, so much the better.

This method puts you in control. You do it your own way. You're active. Not a passive recipient of some magic cure-all. And you can take as long as you want. Just set yourself on a path and don't waver. Challenge yourself. You're playing the long game. Even if you go out for drinks and have a few extra cigarettes, it doesn't mean you failed. Just pick up the next day and keep going. That's the problem with how we think. We're always looking for the quick fix, the instant miracle cure. This mindset is imbedded in American culture. Just take this miracle drug! Works like magic! Guaranteed results! And when we don't get the promised results, we give up, because obviously it didn't work. It's always all or nothing.

There's power in knowing you don't have to succumb to every urge, as opposed to the powerlessness you feel when you have to give it up all at once. Not that the gums and patches don't help. They can deliver the same kind of step-down process of sending less and less nicotine into your system, but you still lose your friends immediately, and all the fun of smoking. And that plays tricks on your mind. You're more likely to rip off the stupid patch, or spit out the gum, and have a smoke. We all want what we can't have. And as Americans we're used to getting any damn thing we want, whenever we want it.

Obviously, this isn't the only way to do it. A friend of mine quit with hypnosis. It comes down to what works for you. This worked for me. In the interest of full disclosure, I quit 10 years ago. But a recent article by a professor and quitting expert noted that tobacco companies have re-engineered cigarettes by increasing the nicotine content, which might make this method tougher. He also noted that he'd seen much more success via cold turkey than gradual cessation.

That may be. He's got stats. My experience was personal. All I know is that detoxing made it easier to quit, as I was fighting my body less and less. And as I felt the cravings begin to subside, the thought entered my head that the cigarettes I thought were my friends were, in fact, my enemy. And they were out to kill me. It helped change my mindset, as I started to examine the emotional and psychological motivations behind my smoking. That also helped get rid of it. In the end, the way you quit smoking should be as unique to you as the reasons you started. It all comes down to knowing yourself.

There was a time I couldn't imagine life without my cigarettes. I'd leave the house and pat the inside pocket of my jacket just to make sure my friends were with me. Now, I can't imagine sucking that acrid smoke back into my body. I think my lungs are clear. I hope there's no nicotine time bomb waiting to go off. But the fact is you can get rid of this addiction without losing your mind. I did. So ends the self-help portion of this book.

CHAPTER TEN

DUMBF✶CKISTAN: THE FUTURE

*"America will never be destroyed from
the outside. If we falter and lose our freedoms,
it will be because we destroyed ourselves."*
Abraham Lincoln

Now that I've trashed American culture, movies, food, politics, and religion, what's left? Maybe puppies and ice cream. At this point you might be thinking: if you think this country's so dumb, leave. You secede. Sorry, I like it here. We've got tons of food, not all of it crap. People are starving all over the world, and we've got 20 different kinds of Pepperidge Farm cookies. Half the world's wiping their asses with their hands, and we've got toilet paper that comes in Sensitive, Ultra Soft, Ultra Strong, with Vitamin E, and scented with Aloe or Chamomile. No wonder the terrorists hate us. Plus, the weather's decent, depending on where you live, and whether it's hurricane or tornado season. In L.A., we've got year-round sunshine, albeit with fire season, a current drought, and the occasional earthquake.

Being American is a nice deal. We're free to follow our dreams and speak our minds. "Love it or leave it" is still better than love it or get thrown in a gulag. Or disappeared in the middle of the night and end up in a stack of bodies piled like cordwood under a soccer stadium. Even with the modified Patriot Act and Snowden revelations about NSA spying, we don't have the Secret Police knocking on the door. We don't get arrested for playing anti-government punk. We may trash political opponents with negative ads and lies, but we don't gun them down in public, or poison them with Polonium 210 slipped into their tea.

Sure, we've had a few assassinations, and a few more attempts, but when it's time for presidents to leave office, they leave. No coups. No show trials. No death sentences. No angry mobs tearing them apart. Just pack up, move out, and start writing your memoir, building your library, and collecting those speaking fees.

We've had political scandals, but the system does self-cleanse. And while the relationship between money and power has gotten even more incestuous in a post-*Citizens United* world, we're still essentially a democracy. We don't have dictators, emperors for life, or military strongmen in army costumes and Ray Bans whose only reason for living is to out-kill and out-crazy their predecessor.

We've also had our wars, both noble and ignoble. We've meddled in the internal politics of a few countries. Propped up the occasional dictator. Assassinated a head of state or two. But considering what the rest of the world's been up to, we're not that bad. In just the last century Europe nearly obliterated itself twice when the war to end all wars didn't. Other highlights include the Armenian genocide, (1.5 million dead), the Holocaust (6 million dead), and the Cambodian killing fields (3 million dead).

And, so far, this century has been no less homicidal. Atheist bloggers are being hacked to death in Bangladesh. Boko Haram terrorists kidnap children and brainwash them into being suicide bombers. (I can barely get my kids to put on a jacket when it's cold out. I can't imagine how tough it would be to zip one of them into a suicide vest. Not that I haven't considered it.) Despite Cher's military advice, ISIS is still cutting heads off, shooting up major cities and blowing up Russian airliners. (I get them screwing with the west. But messing with Putin?

They must be suicidal.) Both the U.S. and the Russians are bombing Syria, we just can't agree on whom to bomb. Heavily armed drug gangs are rampaging all over Mexico, Latin America, and Africa. Sure, we have gangs and gang violence, but no paramilitary armies leaving headless bodies in the street.

We've got Aaron Osmond saying that education shouldn't be mandatory, and Rick Santorum declaring that early childhood education is indoctrination. But no one here is shooting little girls in the head or throwing acid in their faces for the crime of wanting to go to school. Our theocrats just say stupid shit. They're not armed. They're just intellectually dangerous.

Even though Americans murder each other more than any civilized nation, we've still managed to stay above the homicidal mania and mass psychosis consuming much of the world. Our faults aside, if you step outside yourself and see the country through the eyes of someone who risked their life to get here, it gets petty to nitpick. No Americans are paying *coyotajes* to smuggle them across the border into Tijuana.

I was going to title this "Stillbirth of a Nation," just for snark value, but I didn't. Because I don't think that's the case. Despite what I wrote in the intro, America is not retarded. It's a great country. Just, on occasion, a very stupid place, usually when we're all caught up in some national insanity and not living up to the responsibility of being Americans. Slavery -- not our best moment. Prohibition -- bad move, leaving a nasty criminal class hangover. McCarthyism -- yeah, we really lost it, then. But there's an ebb and flow to our stupidity. And even though, over the past 7 years, we've had a very heavy flow, it does seem to be abating. Martin Luther King said that the arc of the moral universe bends toward justice. The same could be said for the arc of American history. It also bends toward reason, and sanity. But it's a slow, slow bend. And with every movement forward, dumb America has shrieked and howled like a wounded animal.

Since the Affordable Care Act was signed into law in 2010, it's been manhandled more than a drunk girl at a frat party, but it's still the law. Socially, we're finally growing up. The Supreme Court has declared gay marriage legal. Though in 2015, the Governors of Texas and Louisiana were threatening to resist that decision, and a Texas pastor threatened to set himself on fire to stop it. Of course, at that point, the only words that come to mind are, "who's got a light?" We're inching toward marijuana legalization and maybe even a re-think on the drug wars and mandatory sentencing, now that we have the distinction of having the highest incarceration rate in the world: 716 people for every 100,000. And while the PC police can occasionally be too hyper-vigilant, looking for racists under every bed, it's positive that we've become intolerant of intolerance.

The Tea Party is still alive and squealing, though soon they won't have Barack Obama to kick around anymore. And while a *Huffington Post* article noted that only 17% of Americans polled say they support the movement, the House Freedom Caucus continues to rage against gays, immigrants, gun control, and

Planned Parenthood. And they're still hell-bent on repealing Obamacare, holding government hostage and/or shutting it down. It's interesting, or actually more disturbing, how they carry themselves with the same self-righteousness and messianic zeal as the terrorists they claim to revile. Tea Partiers, just like terrorists, *kamikaze* pilots, and The Blues Brothers absolutely believe they're on a mission from God. And they're just as willing to blow shit up.

After the Charleston shooting, Governor Nicky Haley was state-shamed into taking down the confederate flag. This was met with a Klan rally on the statehouse grounds, where the Great Titan of the Pelham, North Carolina chapter of the KKK said, "The confederate flag is being took down for all the wrong reasons." Racism and fractured grammar, they go together like grits and gravy.

Of course, sometimes, social change requires political motivation. And it didn't hurt for Haley to come off reasonable, as she's obviously on a short list of Republican Vice Presidential picks. That's why she delivered the GOP rebuttal to the 2016 State of the Union address. Having a woman on the ticket would be an effective counterstrategy against Hillary.

Alabama has also taken down the confederate flag. In Tennessee, Virginia, Maryland, and North Carolina the flag is being removed from license plates. Even Mississippi has acknowledged that it seems to carry some offense. The New Orleans city council has declared confederate-era monuments "a nuisance," and stated their intention to remove them. One hundred and fifty years after Appomattox, and still it takes nine people getting gunned down in church for folks to stop and think that maybe all this Civil War detritus might pour salt in some wounds, while legitimizing hatred in unsound minds. Another step in Southern racism's long, slow death rattle, a process that seems to move as slowly as the South itself, especially with what seems like daily reminders that we've yet to flush this poison from our system.

We've made progress over the years, albeit slow progress. But the unfortunate aspect of every movement for civil rights is that no one in the U.S. should ever have to fight for their civil rights. There never should have been a need for a civil rights movement for the simple reason that the United States *is* a civil rights movement. The extent to which we forget that is the extent to which we haven't lived up to our promise.

Ultimately, the problem isn't America. The problem is Americans, because too many of us are not up to the task of being American. Freedom of speech carries the responsibility of thought. And we don't think. For all our gushing about living in a country dedicated to the proposition that everyone is entitled to life, liberty, and the pursuit of happiness, we don't respect life, we don't understand liberty, and we have a perverted sense of happiness.

LIFE, LIBERTY, HAPPINESS

"The point of dancing is to dance.
Not to end up at a particular spot on the floor."
Alan Watts

It's a strange irony that, as obsessed as we Americans are with our lives, we really don't live all that well. Yes, we have aloe-scented toilet paper. But there's a difference between standard of living and quality of life. And that's where we fall short. We're fat, stressed out, pissed off, heavily armed, jacked up on crappy, fatty food, colored sugar water, drugs, and lousy beer. We work 'til we drop, take little time off, and have no problem if someone gets fired and loses everything. "Hey, tough break. Glad it ain't me." We're one of only two countries in the world without maternity or paternity leave, or any sense of why that might be important for parents, or children. And when we do retire, it's often to planned communities where we play golf, wear tracksuits, and take up drinking and ballroom dancing. Or we take bus tours of Europe, just to remind the rest of the world how classless and clueless we can be.

We also kill each other more than any country in the world. We kill for spite, pride, jealousy, money, parking spaces, gang rivalry, road rage, or just 'cause someone looks at us funny. Or sometimes we just pop off, which is not surprising, considering the pressures of American life. Money, jobs, bills, school. Not just finding the right school, but hoping your kid doesn't get shot during recess.

Our culture not only trades in violence, we celebrate it. Next time you're at the movies check out the trailers. Unless it's a rom-com or some animated kiddie flick, it's all guns, all the time. I recently caught the latest *Star Wars*. Between the *Independence Day* sequel and *The 5th Wave* promos, aliens were blasting the shit out of the planet. Although almost more unsettling was the line from *The 5th Wave*, where the young freedom fighter declares: "This is our world. This is our home. Our only choice is to take it back!" Given the current wave of xenophobia in this country, it had a disturbingly eerie overtone.

We also don't respect the Earth and the ecosystems that sustain it. For years, the greedy, and ultimately suicidal climate change denial movement has tried to block any attempt to deal with the problem. We may not all live in the same neighborhood, but we're all subject to the same weather patterns. And I don't think hurricanes or tornados make exceptions for party loyalty.

As for life itself, we see it as some grand competition, even though, in the human race, ultimately nobody wins. He, who dies with the most toys, still dies. Because of our resistance to introspection, we never ask the question posed in the Platonic dialogues: what is the good life? We don't even have a phrase for it that embodies a national sensibility. The French have *joie de vivre* – joy of life. Italians have *la dolce vita* – the sweet life. The Spanish – *alegria de la vida* – the joy of life.

The Japanese have *mono no aware*, meaning "the pathos of things," an aesthetic grounded in an awareness of the ephemera of life and an appreciation of the present moment. It's an idea inspired by the Buddhist concept of impermanence, and permeates the language and culture, from Haiku poetry to the cherry blossom festival. And the Germans have two words for it. Two! *Lebenslust* and *lebensfreude;* respectfully, zest and love of life. Three countries that pooled their resources in the last century to obliterate civilization have concepts in their culture about enjoying and celebrating life.

The closest we come in America still requires French. *Laissez les bon temps roulez* -- "let the good times roll" -- an expression that embodies the spirit of New Orleans. They celebrate food, music, and life possibly more than anywhere else in the country. They even dance your ass off when you die. Even their national fat ranking should carry an asterisk because it's the result of a lot of gumbo, *etouffee*, Jambalaya, Muffulettas, Po-Boys, *Beignets,* and Hurricanes. No wonder Bush and company were ready to let it drown when Katrina hit; too much life goin' on.

But, what about the rest of us? How do we describe our lives in America? The rat race; the daily grind; the hamster wheel; get rich or die tryin'. We've reduced the good life to a fat ass bank account, and a big ass Mercedes parked in front of an ugly ass McMansion. The good life is the rich life. And in the ultimate act of spiritual contortionism and conceptual spoon bending, we think it's all been given the prosperity gospel seal of approval.

And who's our symbol of success? Donald Trump, the very model of a modern major asshole. Once again, this bloviating idiot has thrown his hair in the presidential ring. And despite the seemingly endless river of racist and sexist bile that's gushed from his mouth and sent him steamrolling toward his party's nomination, he's hardly been the only clown in the GOP presidential circus.

THE 2016 ELECTION

A BATTLE FOR THE
HEART, MIND, AND SOUL
OF AMERICA

In 1960, my father took me to the Commack Arena on Long Island to see John F. Kennedy on a campaign stop. I was one of those kids perched on his dad's shoulders, straining to get a glimpse of the candidate who seemed to represent a new generation of bright, young people coming into government, inspiring hope for the future. Yet, despite the irony in David Halberstam's use of the phrase "the best and the brightest," a half century later the back door of government has been flung open to allow in the worst and the dumbest.

The 2016 presidential election is a battle for the heart, mind, and soul of America. A little melodramatic, I know, but, along with the presidency, the Senate is back in play and, with Scalia's death, the balance of power on the Supreme Court. One swing vote decided *Citizens United*, weakened the Voting Rights Act, allowed religious organizations to opt out of providing coverage for contraception, legalized gay marriage and, in an upcoming case, could render a decision that would virtually gut public-sector unions. That delicate pendulum has swung back and forth, and Scalia's replacement will set this course of this country for generations. And Republicans know that. Terrified that the loss of their conservative stalwart would effectively crush their social and political agenda, they instantly tried to roadblock any nominee by hiding behind the pathetic, transparent talking point of "let the American people decide." The president called their bluff and nominated Merrick Garland, a moderate. And now, the game is on.

It's fascinating to watch Republicans dress up a selfish political agenda in the language of constitutional responsibility. It almost makes me wish Jesus would return, just so President Obama could nominate him for the Court. It would be amusing to watch Republican heads explode as they struggled with the dilemma of party loyalty versus eternal damnation.

Just as in 2008, Hillary has been the presumptive Democratic nominee and, as such, the attacks against her started early. Despite being hammered by Republicans, and Fox News flogging it daily, the 2014 Benghazi hearings didn't accomplish their goal, and that seemed to be the end of that. Until late 2015, when the committee took another shot at her over Benghazi, and her emails. Of course, this was all just a political hit job to get her poll numbers down. This was confirmed when the presumptive new Speaker of the House, Kevin McCarthy, bragged about it on Fox, and was subsequently backed up by another Republican member of the committee, as well as by one of the investigators. Still, that didn't stop Republicans from grilling her for 11 hours, mustering all the faux outrage they could over "four dead Americans!" Unfortunately, for them, she didn't crack. No oops moment. No perjury. No political damage.

In 2015 we also had the Clinton CGI fundraising scandal, which flamed out. Then Republicans floated an ageism attack, but it didn't seem to have any legs, not even old veiny ones, because old people vote, and that most likely pissed them off. And the GOP has pissed off enough people. Not to mention that Hillary is 69, the same age as Ronald Reagan when he was elected.

Republican efforts to pick a nominee have (mostly) been under the guidance of the Chairman of the Republican National Committee, Reince Priebus, whose name is a partial anagram for both *rube penis and pubic sneer*. At least former RNC Chairman Michael Steele delivered the party line with some style, intelligence and wit, as he continues to do as a political commentator. But one look at Priebus and you know his mission in life is to get even with every bully who stuffed him in a gym locker, and every woman who shot him down when all he wanted was a handy behind the bleachers.

After their 2012 loss, Priebus issued a 100-page autopsy analyzing the reasons for their defeat. The stated goal was to be more inclusive, and to reach out to African-American, Asian, Hispanic, and gay voters. Yet, true to form, their takeaway was not to broaden their message, but to shape-shift the messenger. That meant delivering the same policies via browner spokespeople. That's why was Bobby Jindal was picked to do the Republican rebuttal to President Obama's first State of the Union address. It was a cynical GOP ploy. Their way of saying, "You got one; well, we got one, too." In 2013 they gave Marco Rubio a shot, until he caught a case of on-air dry mouth. Not that it mattered, as his oratory style had all the charm of a captive reading a ransom note. With Hillary running, Fiorina jumped in, in an attempt to put a pretty face on the party. But no matter how they dressed it up, it was still just old swine in new bottles.

Despite the economic catastrophe of 2008, and the petri dish of GOP policies that is Kansas, and Louisiana, every single Republican candidate has been hell-bent on pursuing the same course of cutting taxes for the rich, gutting or privatizing social programs that have sustained us for generations, eliminating government agencies, neutering unions, and squeezing the middle class out of existence. What's baffling is that they still can't figure out that this shit may work locally in the off years but you can't run on it nationally if you want the White House. You can play to the hicks in the primaries but eventually the nominee will have to tack to the middle without pissing off the base and terrifying swing voters. And that is one tough high-wire act.

Back in 2009, when Al Franken narrowly won election to the Senate, Senator James Snowball Inhofe, cracked, "Looks like we're going to get the clown from Minnesota." I remember thinking at the time, if the subject is "clowns in the senate," then Al Franken has some pretty big shoes to fill. Unfortunately, since then, it's only gotten worse, a fact made sadly evident by the gaggle of liars, messiahs, and megalomaniacs vying for the GOP presidential nomination.

Starting in mid 2015 the field began growing faster than Duggars, with 17 declared candidates. By March 2016, it had been whittled down to 3. First, let's give a shout-out to the dropout class:

Jeb Bush. Once the presumed frontrunner, Jeb just couldn't get any traction, even after amassing a tremendous war chest, and being rolled out as Jeb! Not the Dumb One! Meanwhile, several neocons wrote books about the Iraq War and embarked on their Magical Revisionist History Tours, all to enable Jeb to distance himself from the sins of his brother. But navigating those waters proved difficult for the heir apparent, as he stumbled right out of the gate. He just couldn't seem to open his mouth without sticking a silver foot in it. And then, he got Trumped. For all his sad attempts to stand up for himself, he was ripped to shreds by the insult comic/candidate. You almost had to feel sorry for the guy as he announced his withdrawal, with that sad bastard look on his face. It was like he was staring in the window of his frat house, not understanding why he couldn't get into the keg party he assumed he'd be hosting.

Marco Rubio. A guy who not only looked uncomfortable in his big boy suit; he looked uncomfortable being alive. After a few debate stumbles, he descended to Trump's level, momentarily turning the primary into a "your mama's so fat" slam-fest and dick-measuring contest, none of which ultimately helped him win his home state. He tanked in Florida, dropped out of the race, and then slinked back to the Senate with his tail between his legs. Based on his attendance record, I'm guessing he needed GPS to find the Capitol Building.

Ben Carson. Huckabee may namedrop Jesus, but Carson actually thought he was Jesus. Carson was Trump on Lithium, saying incredibly stupid shit, but softly. Like criticizing victims in the Oregon school shooting for not rushing the shooter, saying, "He can't get you all." Actually, thanks to Republican opposition to a ban on assault weapons, a shooter with an AR-15 can, in fact, "get you all." After a brief surge in Iowa, and some narcoleptic debate performances, Carson wheezed his way into the final five, before dropping out.

Chris Christie. Government's answer to Tony Soprano; the New Jersey tough guy. And America likes tough guys. Though I don't think his Vegas debate threat to shoot down Russian jets and risk WWIII brought him any converts. Plus, we also like our presidents thin. No one was pining for the second coming of Howard Taft. Bush was an idiot, but at least he was a telegenic idiot.

Carly Fiorina. She came back for a second shot, sporting that eerie, crooked smile that made it look she just ate a bad burrito. She got some momentary visibility with her terse response to Trump's crack about her face, but then vanished back into oblivion, despite her Oscar-worthy performance art piece about Planned Parenthood selling baby parts.

Rick Santorum. A guy who's just a pointy hat and pair of buckled shoes away from being a judge at the Salem witch trials.

Rand Paul. Weird hair and way too beady eyed. Paul came out against getting into more wars, hoping that would play to young people. But, as with his father, his anti-war stance was basically misdirection to turn voters' attention away from his stated goal of destroying social programs so that the poor can pursue their God-given right to starve and die.

Mike Huckabee. Preacher in chief? Not this time. Even though he flashed that good ol' boy, shit-eatin' grin, and turned on the folksy charm, no one was down with his gun-loving, gay-hating Jesus.

Rick Perry. W's shitkicker cousin, with smarty-pants glasses.

Scott Walker. The chinless, beady-eyed, union-busting Wisconsin Governor, and Koch Brothers' tool.

Lindsey Graham. The Senator from Tara.

George Pataki. Former New York Governor, and a guy who permanently sported the self-satisfied grin of someone who just threw poison hamburger in his neighbor's yard to stop the damn dog from barking.

Bobby Jindal. Whatever the opposite of charisma is, he's got it. How can you be Governor of Louisiana and have absolutely no style, wit, or soul? He almost made you pine for the larcenous behavior of some of his predecessors, but Jindal didn't even seem to have the imagination to steal.

Jim Gilmore. The former Virginia Governor. For all the impact he made, I'm guessing this guy was a superhero whose power was invisibility.

All that was missing from the field was Newt, the three-time divorced, family values moralist, and the adulterous pizza guy. Among those remaining in the axis of evil:

Ted Cruz. Cruz's permanent smirk and upturned jaw make him look like Mussolini with a turd under his nose. Supposedly a college debate champ, you can see the sneaky glint in his eye when he thinks he's blown a factitious little lie past an opponent, or the press. It's also ironic that the guy who wants to be the most important person in government gets a boner at the prospect of shutting it down. Cruz bragged that he'd "carpet bomb ISIS into oblivion." Maybe he just got a rush of Testosterone and the comment flew out of his mouth before he remembered that carpet bombing is a war crime, per the 1977 Protocol I, Article 85, Section 3 addition to the Geneva Conventions. So much for his credibility as commander in chief. As of late 2015, he was riding Trump's flatulent wake, hoping to rope-a-dope his way to the nomination, but that strategy soon proved inoperative. Now that Rubio's out, he's trying to make his case as the only candidate who can take on Trumpenstein.

John Kasich. Popular wisdom had Kasich as the reasonable one of the group. Despite an affable persona, he still skulks across a stage like a zombie Nixon. He seemed close to dropping out, until he won his home state of Ohio. Now, it seems he'll hang in. Whether he makes it to the convention or eventually bails, he could easily reappear as a VP choice.

And then there's Trump.

TRUMP

Donald J. Trump. A man who personifies everything that's crude, arrogant, garish, and classless about America. Not class, as in social class, class, as in character. His early speeches were essentially schoolyard taunts against his critics and opponents, and bragging about his poll numbers, all punctuated by phony tough-talk, profanity, silly voices, and stupid faces. The only thing missing from his rallies was a line of elephants walking in circles behind him, their trunks curled around each other's tail.

His policies, if they can be called that, have ranged from the moronic to the ridiculous. He's going to build an 1800-mile fence along the Mexican border, and get Mexico to pay for it. He's going to charge the Mexican government $100,000 for every illegal immigrant. How, toll booth? He's going to round up and deport 11 million undocumented immigrants, humanely; sort of like kicking someone in the balls, compassionately. His tax plan would add $11.2 trillion to the national debt by 2026, and $34.1 trillion by 2036. He's going to fight ISIS by "bombing the shit out of them." He's going to force the estimated 5-8 million Muslims living in the United States to carry ID cards. Then, puffing out his chest like the Mayor of Munchkinland, he unfurls a proclamation calling for a ban on Muslims coming into the country. Does he really think that any terrorist who's determined enough to come here and blow himself up would shy away from lying about his religious affiliation? What's he going to do, force every Middle Eastern immigrant to eat a hot dog at the border?

As for his immigration plan, frankly, I'm a little disappointed with the wall idea. It's very un-Trump-like. The Trump I know would build an 1800-mile *Trump Golf and Tennis Resort* along the border, and put the wall on the American side. This way, the non-rapist Mexicans could work there during the day, and go back home at night, so no one can sneak into the country. Though they still could get on a path to citizenship by putting in years of service and accumulating *Trumppoints* (™). After accruing a certain amount of points, they could apply for work permits and, eventually move here and live on this side of the wall. This would give Trump and his team of experts time to weed out "the good ones." So, all the men would have to do to become American citizens is mix Daiquiris or rake sand traps for, say, 10 years. And all the women would have to do is blow him.

Trump claims to be "very presidential." Right. Of all the inspirational language candidates have used to announce a run for the presidency, I've heard "hope," "change," "vision," "American dream," and "shining city on a hill." No one I can recall has ever used the word "rapists." And he's definitely the first to pile a stack of meat on a table during a primary victory speech. Of course, after Rubio's "tiny hands" crack, the intention behind the meat stack was very clear. If he were overcompensating any more, Trump Tower would have a foreskin on top.

Yet, despite all this insane, irrational, childish behavior, despite racist comments about Mexicans and African-Americans, sexist cracks about women, veiled threats against reporters, and inciting violence against protesters, he's winning primaries and piling up delegates, hoping to steamroll his way to the nomination.

Many who try to comprehend Trump's popularity suggest that he's tapped into an electorate that's pissed off about the economy and Washington gridlock. Bullshit. What he's tapped into is the apoplexy of people who feel emasculated by the fact that we elected a black president, then re-elected the black president, and then didn't impeach the black president for the high crime of being president while black. Trump's people aren't worked up about his policies. They're exhilarated over the possibility of being re-empowered. Check out the crowd at his rallies? Notice any political scientists, economists, or policy wonks? Nope, just a bunch of dumb, angry white people, falling under the sway of an egomaniacal megalomaniac.

It's not what Trump says that gets the crowd riled up. It doesn't matter what he says. It's how he says it. His candidacy is McLuhanesque. The medium is the message. He could bark out the first chapter of *Das Kapital* and his audience would stand up and cheer. His supporters don't know what he's talking about because he doesn't know what he's talking about. One look in his eyes and you can see he's just spewing out the nastiest, most provocative shit that enters his head. In FDR's 1933 inaugural address, he calmed a nation in the throes of the Great Depression, saying: "… the only thing we have to fear is fear itself…" What do we get from Trump? "Be afraid! Be very afraid!"

It's not that he's playing to the Republican base. It's that he is the Republican base. He's dumb. Trump is Rich White Trash. Yes, I know he says: "I went to the best schools. I'm very smart." You know who says, "I'm smart," stupid people who are afraid of getting found out. As for his boast about attending the prestigious Wharton school, some say he only got in because his father gave money to the school and the admissions officer was a friend of his brother's. I'm not saying that. But some people are. Maybe he should release his Fordham transcripts and clear that up. The American people deserve to know the truth. Not that it would matter to his crowd. When he talks, no one's listening to the words. They're swaying to the music.

Remember that New Hampshire rally where the birther regurgitated Trump's anti-Muslim rhetoric, and the candidate didn't shoot him down? The media instantly focused on what Trump didn't say, in that he didn't defend the president's basic human decency, like McCain did in 2008. But forget what Trump didn't say. Look at what he said. He said: "We're gonna be looking at a lot of different things. And you know a lot of people are saying that bad things are happening out there. We're gonna be looking at that, and plenty of other things." Wow. Sounds like something JFK might have said, after the head wound.

Trump may be clever. He may be shrewd. But he's not smart. In fact, he's dumb. The guy's a mook, a dope, a dunsky, a doofus. The Fredo Corleone of the Republican Party. The Forrest Gump of politics. Forrest Trump. Except that Gump was a noble soul who looked for the good in people. Trump calls everyone who challenges him, "losers." Gump had humility. Trump builds gold-plated dick substitutes and sticks his name on them. Gump was in love with one woman. Trump trades in wives like most people trade in car leases. He couldn't even go to Liberty University and pull off his fake Christian act without screwing up the title of a Bible verse. He was even too stupid to pander intelligently.

Still he's rolling up primary victories, and the Republican establishment can't seem to stop him. Nor can the media. Lawrence O'Donnell can excoriate him in a scathing editorial. Louis CK can write a brilliant email. No effect. The *National Review* can gang-bang him. Nothing. Even respected politicians can't neutralize him. Senator Elizabeth Warren delivered a passionate, eloquent takedown, and it just bounced off him like he was Superman, with a comb-over. He wears the attacks as a badge of honor, which only makes his base love him more. As Woody Allen's character in *Manhattan* said in response to a guy talking about a satirical piece in the *New York Times* about Nazis marching in New Jersey, "You can't satirize a guy with shiny boots on."

Some pundits trying to be even-handed say they've been to his rallies and spoken with his people, and they're not just a herd of ignorant racists. Sorry, but no. That's factually incorrect. Trump support is a litmus test for intelligence. No thinking, sentient human being can possibly listen to his speeches, and observe his behavior, and think that this man is presidential.

Even if some of his supporters have been hit by hard times and like the sound of his absurdly simplistic solutions to their problems, the truth is he's conning them. He treats the electorate like a woman he has no respect for, yet still wants to fuck. "You're gonna have so many orgasms, it's gonna be amazing, fantastic, incredible! Your head's gonna spin!" This billionaire doesn't give a shit about making their lives better. He's not bringing millions of jobs back to America. He doesn't have the knowledge, or the experience to know how these things get done. He's in it for his bloated ego. Like the carnivorous plant in *Little Shop of Horrors*, he stands there barking, "Feed me!"

Donald Trump is Dumbfuckistan incarnate. Just as Sarah Palin was its head cheerleader, Trump is its star quarterback. It was hardly surprising that she showed up in Iowa to endorse him, delivering a speech that made her sound like a drunken stroke victim. They made quite a pair, standing on stage: the unstoppable farce meets the unshameable object.

Trump's primary success is living proof of the dumbing down of the country, and to his ultimate stupidity, because even if he manages to get the nomination, he'll most likely get thumped in the general election. He may be popular with the poorly educated, but eventually, he'll need the votes of everyone he's pissed off. You can't run for the presidency by alienating women,

African-Americans, Latinos, Asians, Muslims and, frankly, anyone with a barely functioning cerebral cortex. Every word that's come out of his mouth has given Democrats a virtual Bartlett's book of quotations they can beat him with in attack ads.

At the moment, he's too afraid to sit for an interview that isn't a political reach-around, but that strategy won't fly in a general election. He won't be able to duck the press forever. He'll have to handle real questions, and real follow-up questions.

He's bragged about how badly he'd beat Hillary in a debate. And his supporters are eager to watch their champion in action. And that may be his Waterloo, because going one-on-one against her, Trump will get clobbered or, in his parlance – schlonged. He won't be able to talk policy with any measure of substance, or intelligence. She'll beat him silly with facts, and then he'll get flustered, turn red (well, redder), and lose his shit, because, along with being dumb, Trump is also a pussy. He can dish it out on Twitter, but he can't take it. He can't deal with being attacked, especially by a woman. Eventually, he'll do the only thing that could turn off his base: he'll look weak. And he's not smart enough to see any of this coming, which proves that the man is an idiot, or has just been dicking us around, because he could have been president.

Instead of making his debut spitting racist attacks and bad insult comic shots, all he had to do was tout his success as a businessman, negotiator, and job creator. He could have borrowed a page from Reagan and blown some "shining city on a hill" up our asses. He could've explained the bankruptcies by saying he knew what it felt like to get knocked down and get back up again. Even though he was born with a silver spoon up his ass, that message might have resonated with a broader audience; i.e. swing voters. He could've said more benign versions of everything he's saying now, and appealed to the same base, while even enticing his version of Reagan Democrats. He could have appealed to the best in us, instead of pandering to the worst in us.

Of course, it would have involved some degree of reinvention, as he was already knee deep in birtherism. And there's his history of infantile Twitter wars. LBJ fought the war on poverty. Bush fought the war on terror. Trump fought the war on Rosie O'Donnell. Then there was that time he referred to the Chinese as "motherfuckers." I'm not sure how that expression translates into Mandarin, but I'm guessing it doesn't come off as a compliment.

Trump could have made an attempt to reinvent himself, but he didn't. Instead, he went the goon route, throwing red meat to the base, all while sporting facial expressions that made him look like he was the one with the disability. And now he's gone from buffoonish, to despicable, to dangerous, with the claim that his people will riot if he's denied the nomination at a brokered convention; a virtual dog whistle call to arms for his more rabid supporters to commit violence. And they will respond. Cleveland '16 could be a repeat of Chicago '68, but with guns.

I know there's Godwin's Law, and the notion that the moment Hitler is invoked in an argument, the argument is lost. So I won't compare Trump to Hitler. He's more Hitler-Lite. Although if it came down to a decision between Trump and Cruz over whose hand I would prefer on the nuclear button, I'd have to go with Trump. The man's rich. He obviously relishes the pleasures of this life. Cruz is a religious fanatic who thinks there's a better time awaiting in the sky. He's in a hurry to get to the next world, so why not blow this one up.

For most Americans, the election of the first African-American president was a milestone in correcting a 350-year-old crime. It was a cleansing moment, and a sign of hope for the future. But for others it was a moment of fear, and Republicans played on that for 7 years, insidiously fomenting anger, mistrust, and outright hatred. Now, they bemoan the loss of their party. Well, tough shit. You cynically picked the scab of racism until the wound opened and the pus called Trump oozed out. You birthed this monstrous idiot. You deal with him.

These are serious times. And serious times call for serious people. It's one thing to play the renegade and flaunt the established norms of the political process. Politics is a dirty business. The higher you go, the dirtier it gets. But no matter how pissed off we get during the elections, no matter how cynical we may be about the process, ultimately we never fall out of love with our ideals. Trump's dumb thug routine is in the worst tradition of demagoguery in this country. It demeans the presidency, itself. Eventually, this will bite him in the ass.

As for the non-Trump Republicans' road to the White House, the tollbooth is still manned by the Koch brothers and the reported $1 billion they're ready to spend to buy a president. In early 2015, when he thought he had a shot at some of that cash, Rand Paul delivered a speech, talking about the Koch brothers' "passion for freedom." And what, exactly, is that passion? In 1980 David Koch ran for Vice President on the Libertarian Party ticket. He got hammered, which lead him to take a more behind-the-scenes role in politics. But, at the time, this was his take on the America he'd like to see, as expressed in his platform:

Repeal all federal campaign finance laws.

Abolish Medicare and Medicaid.

Opposition to any plan to provide health services.

Deregulate the medical insurance industry.

Repeal Social Security.

Abolish the Postal Service.

Repeal all taxation, personal and corporate.

Repeal any and all minimum wage laws.

End all government ownership, operation, regulation and subsidy of schools and colleges.

End all compulsory education laws.

Abolish the EPA.

Abolish the Department of Energy.

Abolish the Department of Transportation.

Abolish the FAA, FDA, and OSHA.

Abolish the Consumer Product Safety Commission.

Opposition to laws requiring individuals to buy or use safety belts, air bags or crash helmets.

Opposition to all government programs, or relief projects that aid the poor.

What kind of country does that sounds like to you? Utopia? Or Mad Max Fury Road? And the Kochs have not backed off that stance. Nor have the culture warriors. The Republican rallying cry of the last seven years has been that they want to take the country back. Yes, back to a time when men worked and women stayed home and watched the kids. A time when there were no drugs but everyone drank. There were no abortions except in back alleys. No gays, except in the closet. Minorities knew their place. And strikers got their heads busted. And if we didn't like another country, we bombed the shit out of it; their whitewashed, utopian dream, and every else's dystopian nightmare. That's why they won't be able to buy this election. For all the money infecting the process, they still have to sell their policies, and that will be their undoing. Because those policies run counter to one very basic reality: human life.

It should be self-evident that there are basic needs for life: food, clothing, shelter, education, work, and health care. This isn't a matter of opinion. It's fact. We all need to eat. We don't run around naked. People don't live outside. Well, some do, but not by choice. Most of us agree that education is a good thing. We should all get fulfillment from work but, at the end of the day, we've got to put food on the table. In time, we get old and retire. And when we get old and retire is also when we tend to get sick. And then we die. We don't all get sick and die. Sometimes we just die. Or we shoot each other and die. Not just Democrats. Republicans die as well. Any political system or society that doesn't take into account the inevitability of disease at a time when people are retired or living on a fixed income; or worse, if someone in a family gets sick at a young age, is not dealing with life. It's not just American life, or Democrat life. It's actual life.

Fighting any attempt to make health care more available is to assert that the value of a human life should be based on an economic model of profit and loss, and an insurance company's stock price. In short, it's ok if some people go broke and die. It's survival of the richest. No one's saying that the rich can't indulge themselves with the best medical care. That's the way we do it here. If you can pay for it, you can get it. But a system that offers premium care for the few doesn't have to simultaneously begrudge basic care for the many. Particularly given the traditional business model of insurance companies, which is that you're covered for everything except what happens to you.

To refer to Medicare, Medicaid, and Social Security as entitlements carries the pejorative implication that people are taking something to which they have no right. But it should be the moral choice of a society or government that everyone has that right. "Right to life." Isn't that the expression? It should also exist after a person is born.

Another way to look at these battles is in Freudian terms. Our politics is essentially a war with ourselves, the natural extension of our conflicting psychological impulses. The id gives us Republicans, who value individual rights and resist any impediment to a person pursuing their self-interest. (Unless of course it involves sex. In which case the government must step in and the guilty must be slut-shamed.) Our superego gives us Democrats, who value the role of government and our responsibility to one another. And, like an individual with a healthy ego, we need both aspects of who we are to live life to the fullest. That's why we have a Defense Department, and Medicare.

Before John Edwards literally screwed himself out of his political life, he ran on the slogan that there were two Americas: rich and poor. But in the last seven years, we've also divided ourselves into smart America and dumb America. And as someone who prefers to live in smart America I'm making a plea to the GOP: If there are any limited government, old-fashioned values, strong defense, honest day's work for an honest day's pay types left, please stand up for reason and reclaim your party. Kick out the clowns. Lose the hysteria. And the racism. Instead of trading on hate and fobbing it off as dissent, denounce the lunatics and rejoin the legitimate debate.

And if what's needed are some breadcrumbs on the path to find your way back, here's a start: the 1956 election, a rematch of 1952, pitting Democrat Adlai Stevenson against ultra-liberal Dwight Eisenhower, and his running mate, that raging socialist Richard Nixon. Here are some excerpts from the Republican platform:

- Provide federal assistance to low-income communities.
- Protect social security.
- Provide asylum for refugees.
- Extend the minimum wage.
- Improve the unemployment benefit system so it covers more people.
- Strengthen labor laws so workers can easily join a union.
- Assure equal pay for equal work regardless of sex.

And while that wasn't the entirety of the platform, every one of these points has become Republican heresy. Ultimately, there will always be greedy bastards in life, and it doesn't matter which political party, economic philosophy or religious tradition they hide behind. And there will always be well-intentioned people on either side of the argument, who simply come at life from different perspectives, ones that are rooted in the conflicting impulses in the human mind and the human heart. Until we get down to first principles, and examine these ideas in light of a government's responsibility, the debates will rage on. Unfortunately, these days, the debates are mostly raging. Civilized discourse has become almost non-existent. Sadly, as we descend even further into the black hole of insults, race-baiting, negative ads, opposition research, scandals, and congressional show trials, any hope for an intelligent national dialogue that might actually lead to finding solutions to our problems seems fleeting.

I started writing this in 2011. It's now early 2016, and I'm done. Ranted out. Even though we have miles to go before the election, I'm going back to being an observer. And while I think Hillary Clinton will be the next President of the United States, I also have to give Bernie Sanders due respect.

In 1964, when Barry Goldwater ran against Lyndon Johnson, he pushed many of the same buttons Trump's pushing now. Goldwater's campaign slogan was: "In your heart, you know he's right." Then, it was a cynical shout-out to our dark side. Now, minus the cynicism, it sums up my feelings about Senator Sanders. In my heart, I know he's right. Ideologically, he's fighting the right battles, and has been consistent throughout his political career in his efforts to make life in this country better for those who are struggling. When I hear him speak, I get the same feeling as when I listen to John Lennon's *Imagine*. Lovely sentiments. It's the way life ought to be. It's just not going to happen, at least not at this stage of our American evolution.

The popular wisdom is that Hillary will win the nomination, and the presidency. However, if there's one thing that's sure in this life, it's that you can go broke betting on the popular wisdom. The only thing predictable about this election is that it's unpredictable. Trump may yet have a few moves up his sleeve should he choose to try to make himself palatable, or less onerous, to swing voters. Plus, there's always the chaos factor. And 2016 started out in full-chaos mode. The Chinese stock market plummeted, sending U.S. markets into a nosedive. Oil prices hit new lows. The North Koreans claimed to have tested an H-bomb.

Given the fact that ISIS is hell-bent on their virgin-stocked after-hours club, it wouldn't take much to throw a figurative, and literal bomb into this election with another 9/11-style attack in the U.S. If that happened, all bets would be off. Republicans would instantly seize on it, beating the drum that Democrats are soft on defense. They'd blame Obama and, by extension, Hillary. They'd wave the fear flag, and not only Republicans would come under its sway, but possibly Democrats as well. Even though Hillary's got more foreign policy experience than any GOP candidate, our ingrained sexism could kick in and we'd look for big daddy to protect us. This is exactly the kind of scenario in which thugs like Trump or Cruz rise to power. And with a Republican in the White House and GOP control of Congress, they'd do everything possible to drag this country back to the Stone Age. Should that happen, I'd probably just take my chances and move to Syria.

And as for those ultra-cynics who like to stand outside the fray and snort, "Why vote? There's really no difference between the parties. Democrats and Republicans are all just whores to Wall Street and big money," consider this: Since leaving the White House, former president Jimmy Carter worked on behalf of Habitat For Humanity. He also formed The Carter Center, which has worked all over the world promoting democracy, monitoring elections, encouraging human rights, access to information, and government transparency. The Center fosters conflict resolution, works for peace in Africa, the Middle East, Latin

America and Asia, and leads the fight against preventable diseases in Africa. In the summer of 2015, President Carter announced that he had been diagnosed with an aggressive form of brain cancer, yet handled the news with about as much dignity and, yes, faith, as anyone I've ever seen.

Since leaving office, Bill Clinton formed the Clinton Global Initiative, which convenes global leaders to explore creative solutions to world problems. They've brought together present and former heads of state, Nobel laureates, and hundreds of CEOs, foundation heads and NGOs. The foundation focuses on global health, increased opportunity for women and girls, creating economic opportunity, and addressing climate change. Through 2014 they'd raised almost $2 billion on behalf of those efforts.

Since leaving the White House in 2008, George Bush took up finger-painting.

AFTERWORD
TRUMPOCALYPSE NOW

It's now mid 2018, two years after this book was published. I thought Hillary would win the election. I was wrong. Trump won.

The election was ultimately about empowerment. Actually, the last two elections were about empowerment, but of a different electorate. Obama's was based on something noble. Trump's on something ignoble -- the resurgence of our semi-dormant, or temporarily shamed racism.

Once upon a time in America even the poorest poor bastard could step out of his trailer, crack open a beer, light up an unfiltered Camel, and take that first deep breath of air that smelled like dog piss and gasoline, but still feel that the world was in its proper place, because what got his ass down to the filling station to clean toilets eight hours a day was the feeling that, as bad as life was, at least he was better off than someone because he was white. But when a black guy got elected president that rationale was gone. And those people were angry. They were confused. And they wanted their country back.

On election night I began writing a follow-up book that I put out in 2017, entitled: *Freak Out: The 2016 Election and the Dawn of the American Democalypse*. It was my take on what happened, and why. I occasionally considered whether it was, in fact, the dawn of our democalypse, or just a temporary swing of the political pendulum. At times I thought it was unnecessarily cynical. Now, I'm not so sure. It all may hinge on the results of the 2018 midterms. I don't think Democrats will take back the Senate. They have a chance of taking control of the House but, as of this writing, it remains an open question whether they can learn not just how to fight, but how to sell their ideas to swing state voters who may be suffering from Trump regret. The wild card may still be the Mueller investigation and whether it becomes the engine of Trump's downfall.

One thing is for certain: Trump will never go down without a fight. And even if he's impeached, or loses the 2020 election, he may just lock himself in the Oval Office and play out the end of Scarface, blasting away with a high-powered rifle, screaming, "Say hello to my little friend!"

Made in United States
North Haven, CT
09 November 2022